Weil Lectures on American Citizenship

DISCIPLINE FOR DEMOCRACY

Weil Lectures on American Citizenship

JACOB H. HOLLANDER
American Citizenship and Economic Welfare

R. GOODWYN RHETT
The Progress of American Ideals

WILLIAM BENNETT MUNRO
Personality in Politics

EDWARD ALSWORTH ROSS
Roads to Social Peace

WILLIAM ALLEN WHITE
Some Cycles of Cathay

HENRY NOBLE MACCRACKEN
John the Common Weal

WILLIAM HEARD KELPATRICK
Our Educational Task

HAROLD J. LASKI
Democracy in Crisis

GEORGE NORLIN
Fascism and Citizenship

FELIX FRANKFURTER
The Commerce Clause

HENRY A. WALLACE
Technology, Corporations, and the General Welfare

T. V. SMITH
Discipline for Democracy

CHAPEL HILL: THE UNIVERSITY OF NORTH CAROLINA PRESS

Discipline for Democracy

T. V. SMITH

Chapel Hill
The University of North Carolina Press
1942

*Copyright, 1942, by
The University of North Carolina Press*

To

NANCY

AND HER COMRADES

IN PATHS
OF
DEMOCRATIC DISCIPLINE

Preface

AT BERLIN it was in the melancholy years following the First World War. It was night, a night in early autumn. The shadows cast before by approaching winter were strangely reminiscent of the deeper shadows retreating slowly with the softening memories of that struggle. We had been arrayed, my host and I, on opposite sides: he an adviser of Emperor and generals, I an obscure private in the hastily gathered forces beyond the sea. Now we were friends, sitting in his study in Berlin.

He pointed to treasured pictures upon the walls. Here was the Emperor himself, an autographed likeness. Here was a general whose name had once stirred pride at home, tremor abroad. Here, there, and yonder hung the pictures of great diplomats—his friends in days already dead though not far gone. He spoke of them with not too much pride and with no trace of apology. The war had been a horrible mistake, yes; but a mistake of all nations, not merely of his own. And yet—he spoke with deep earnestness—it has been in a peculiar sense the mistake of his own nation, of his very friends. They had certainly not meant to cause what came but only to settle a minor international quarrel in a way somewhat high-handed. They had acted in good faith in whatever they did leading up to the war. But they had failed to understand the view that other nations would take of their actions—this had been the fatal mistake for which he wished to acknowledge his share of blame. In a world where no responsible men really want war, this is the type of blame somebody must always take, the blame of failure to understand while yet there is time.

This kind of mistake was preventable, he thought. Indeed he had set himself to raise a bulwark against war, by remedying such ignorance. I saw from his animation that the task was more than duty laid upon him by regret. If once it had been a burden to his conscience, it was now a duty grown into a glad vocation, yea, into a resplendent career. I did not yet perceive the deep springs of his devotion to his new-found cause: that part of his story was to come only with the deepening night.

His school was already on the way to an established success. It was for the training of young diplomats before they took up their work in foreign parts. No longer, indeed, were they being filled with mere blind pride in the superiority of their homeland; no longer fed on suspicion of other lands and peoples. That had been, he repeated, the double story of the old blindness. No; these ambassadors of the future would be filled with knowledge of and touched with feeling for other lands before they went out to represent their own. They would know what other men felt before they coined their own feelings into irrevocable acts. Feeling can be changed by sympathy with the feelings of others; but actions cannot be recalled. As he quietly voiced such stirring, sober sense, the autumn breeze blew chillier through the half-open window, laden with the somber echoes of living millions mourning the millions more whose voices war had stilled.

Yes; actions by diplomats, like actions by other men, were past recall; but emotions were plastic; and insight might be made to take the place of unending regret. My host's enthusiastic tone presently recalled my mind from its morbid pondering amid the recently visited battlefields. Had he not that very day won over to his school the last great opposing group? Hereafter all parties would require this broad training of their ambitious young men. A distinguished American scholar had just concluded his lectures to the school; soon a Japanese statesman would come to visit and to instruct, then a Frenchman—until in two years' time the narrowness of a purely national point of view would give way to fuller humanitarianism. He dreamed indeed of the time when nations would be represented to each other only by men of international minds.

I watched his face as it glowed with pride over what he had achieved, as it filled with hope when he spoke of the future. His story swiftly told, he fell into silence; but a silence out of which more speech, I thought, would presently come. As I watched his face, however, I saw enthusiasm and hope give way to a wistfulness touched now and then by flickers of obvious pain which would almost surely prove too deep for words. I settled to silence though still prepared to brace myself for less pleasant conversation, observing the while his mobile countenance. Suddenly he spoke in tones touchingly softened, as though half apologizing for what he had been saying about himself and his educational exploits.

"The real founder of my school," he gestured, "is there behind you."

Touched by his curious self-control and slightly apprehensive at his gesture to what I had thought empty space behind me, I turned cautiously around to make out in a corner of the room the bronze bust of a handsome youth. It was so near me and yet so remote; so silent and yet so eloquent in that stilled study, that I quailed before its wordless stare. The silence clutched like an accusing apparition.

With infinite relief to me, the father at last called my attention away from the statue, which had fixed me with its poignancy. In my unsteadiness, he had quite recovered himself. It was his only son, he said simply, a youth hardly eighteen, called to the colors two weeks before the armistice and sent at once to his death, without training and with no instructions, the very night before the final truce was called. Unidentified, the body found its way to an unknown grave. The war over, a French corporal discovered the tag of identification; and, exposing himself to discipline for so doing, had notified the father of his discovery. My host had gone at once, had made his way through still hostile territory, and had stood at last before a probable spot that would be to him forever sacred.

When my mind wanders back to Europe blackened by another World War, it can never miss a spot immortalized in purest pathos. My host of those distant days is long a refugee driven from his homeland by its resurgent passion. But his study remains a spot mellowed by memory. That ghostly study is graced still with the statue of a handsome youth. The bronzed apparition speaks no words, but I listen to what it says more intently than to all the guns booming here or to any bombs bursting there. Across the gulf of years memory transports me again into the presence of that youthful symbol; and in its shadow I part again with my host, but now with the vision of that strange night of the long ago. It was a vision that reached beyond the discipline of death; it opened vistas upon another discipline, one that leads to life and to life more abundant.

Oh, Wind, if the winter of mankind's direst discontent be come again, can the Spring of youth's immortal hope be far behind?

T. V. S.

Southern Memorial Day, 1942

Acknowledgments

To the University of North Carolina for the pleasures afforded by a visit to Chapel Hill, and to the Weil Lectureship there for its honorable prompting to put to paper thoughts upon a subject of such intimate importance today; to my own publishers for permission to revive here (without charge) certain paragraphs from books of mine now out of print (to Whittlesy House for paragraphs from *Beyond Conscience* and to the University of Chicago Press for paragraphs from *The Legislative Way of Life*); and to Little, Brown, and Company for permission to quote from *The Poems of Emily Dickinson,* edited by Martha Dickinson Bianchi and Alfred Leete Hampson, the several selections (for $60.00) from this philosophic poet on whose artistic insights I have here so heavily leaned.

T. V. S.

Contents

1
DISCIPLINE: DYNAMIC AND DECADENT
PAGE 1

2
SCIENCE: THE DISCIPLINE OF TRUTH
PAGE 21

3
ART: THE DISCIPLINE OF BEAUTY
PAGE 49

4
POLITICS: THE DISCIPLINE OF GOODNESS
PAGE 91

INDEX
PAGE 133

Overtone

When the effervescence of democratic negation extends its workings beyond the abolition of external distinctions of rank to spiritual things—when the passion for equality is not content with founding social intercourse upon universal sympathy, and a community of interests in which all may share, but attacks the lines of Nature which establish orders and degrees among the souls of men—they are not only wrong, but ignobly wrong. Modesty and reverence are no less virtues of freemen than the democratic feeling which will submit neither to arrogance nor to servility.

To inculcate those virtues, to correct the ignoble excess of a noble feeling to which I have referred, I know of no teachers so powerful and persuasive as the little army of specialists. They carry no banners, they beat no drums; but where they are, men learn that bustle and push are not the equals of quiet genius and serene mastery. They compel others who need their help, or who are enlightened by their teaching, to obedience and respect. They set the examples themselves; for they furnish in the intellectual world a perfect type of the union of democracy with discipline.

—Justice Oliver Wendell Holmes,
Collected Legal Papers.

I

Discipline: Dynamic and Decadent

And God saw everything that He had made, and, behold, it was very bad. On the seventh day, therefore, God could not rest. In the morning and evening He busied Himself with terrible and beautiful concoctions and in the twilight of the seventh day He finished that which is of more import than the beasts of the earth and the fish of the sea and the lights of the firmament. And He called it Imagination . . . for no other reason was imagination given unto us than that we might refashion the Creator's wretched handiwork, that we might remake an ugly universe in the likeness of our dreams.—Russell Gordon Smith, "Fugitive Papers."

BEFORE US TODAY fate has set a fearful choice: this way it is death; that way it is life. Here is a discipline decadent, leading to death; there is discipline dynamic, leading toward the abundant life.[1] The dynamic way is hard of choice, but easier of fulfilment. The decadent way is easy of choice, and impossible of fulfilment.

To speak, however, of dynamic discipline is to suggest a paradox, but a paradox which today represents the predicament of democratic citizenship. A paradox which is also a predicament imposes not so much a quandary as a task. Ours is a task challenging the highest ingenuity and our deepest stamina. Man lives always in a natural world where little worth while can be achieved without its price, without his discipline. "All things excellent," said Spinoza, "are as difficult as they are rare." But men live now in a political world where the very term "dynamic" has been all but reserved for a discipline which dissipates what free men prize. Since we as free men cannot survive without discipline and since survival justifies itself only when touched with the dynamic, we have as the supreme duty of democratic citizenship to minimize the price and to maximize the privileges purchased thereby. An evil which, like discipline, is necessary is, however, never wholly evil. Initially bad, discipline can eventually become a good. It reaches its greatest goodness when it escapes the decadence that always dogs it and achieves the dynamic for which it exists. How far it can do this depends upon time and place, upon populations and their abiding principles.

Let us, however, begin at the beginning of this elemental matter of discipline and unfold as systematically as may be what discipline means, what it necessitates, what it promises. We have a duty to clarify the situation in which the honorable term "dynamic" has been prostituted to the very dregs of decadence, and we accept the privilege of presenting such case as there is for the dynamic nature of democratic citizenship. After a general word upon imagination and its role in life—thus to lift discipline from the picayune to which we pedagogues sometimes condemn it—we shall clear the ground of negatives and proceed to open in the name of our way of life vistas infinitely inspiring.

TRIMMING THE WICK OF IMAGINATION

Imagination is the source of (insight into) the values for which discipline exists as means. It is the mother of all else; yes, and father too. Long before mind became useful as science or beautiful as art, it was and is intriguing as fancy, majestic as aspiration. The mood of reverie is indigenous to man. "Heaven lies about us in our infancy." The child with that far-away look in his eyes has already discovered and under the protective device of detachment is this moment exploring a magic realm where images chase one another rapturously and each *is* for the nonce what later it will only represent. Here is material least of all resistant to desire, and of this material is woven all else that partakes of the ideal.

Let me commend, therefore, if not the theology then the strategy of that cosmic accounting done by the sensitive contemporary quoted at the beginning of this chapter, Russell Gordon Smith. I repeat its moral: "for no other reason was imagination given unto us than that we might refashion the Creator's wretched handiwork, that we might remake an ugly universe in the likeness of our dreams." We must recover something of the roominess of this legend in order to lift discipline from a despised and dangerous status to a lustrous stature for our democracy. We shall not be dynamic without right discipline. We shall grow decadent with wrong discipline. Imagination it is which must be disciplined, but it must be done imaginatively if we are to survive the discipline and prosper from it.

Infancy gives us the makings of all that ever will be right and fine. Childhood so matures the majesty of our inherited make-believe that growth-into-life is likely to every romantic soul to appear a devolution, a fading of the genuinely perfect "into the light of common day." In the Garden of Allah which adolescence is, there is hardly a footfall less expectant than the rustling of an angel's wing. Or if we must have villainy to enhance the glorious, a string is attached to jerk the villain from his infamy at the very point of breath-taking peril. The romantic mood would, Faust-like, hold onto, however hardly it be done, all that is bequeathed through this universal legacy.

In childhood this romantic mood breeds petulance against whatever hinders our grasping the moon; in adolescence it breeds rebellion, as against hypocrisy at every accommodation that the elders have made to life and to one another. In mature life it provokes insistence upon the "ought-to-be" against even complete absence of means to make the "ought" into the "is." Such middle-aged romanticism has of late given to a university graduating class this moral touched at the edges with humor but shot through and through with reflective pathos in an age of war:

"My experience and observation," said President Robert Maynard Hutchins to the graduating class at Chicago, 1935, "lead me to warn you that the greatest, the most insidious, the most paralyzing danger you will face is the danger of corruption. Time will corrupt you. Your friends, your wives or husbands, your business or professional associates will corrupt you; your social, political, and financial ambitions will corrupt you. The worst thing about life is that it is demoralizing. . . . Believe me, you are closer to the truth now than you ever will be again . . . take your stand now before time has corrupted you. Before you know it, it will be too late."

Such anguished perfectionism, reminiscent of adolescence, becomes a sort of ethical onanism in education. In politics it becomes, nationally, disdain for the best that compromise can achieve and, internationally, the isolationism which makes Pearl Harbors easy to occur and very hard to endure. If men are ever to become happily heterogenous as between the ideal and the rugged real, it is with travail of spirit much beyond the innocence of undergraduates and much below the "realism" of isolation. No blaming of Rousseau, or even of the pragmatists, as is the present wont of some romantics of mediaevalism, can make fecund the throb of disillusion or disguise the pains of parturition, however belatedly the pangs of growth may come upon romantics.

Only through maturation of our imaginative powers by the acceptance of their responsibilities, not through adulation of adolescence or innocence of isolation, can a single value be precipitated from bright ideality into the half satisfactions of crass reality. "It is the imagination," observes Sherwood Anderson, "that drives us on, that can destroy us, that sometimes makes a man do heroic deeds, that produces all of our art and poetry, that has produced all inventions that make modern life so strangely different from life a few generations ago." This mother of so much remains mother only through continuing martyrdom. A heart resolute enough to renounce whatever is necessary in order to realize a somewhat that is desirable is the painful condition that discipline lays upon every aspiring soul. It was this to which our judicial sage pointed when, in writing his friend, Sir Frederick Pollock, Justice Holmes gave birth to this moral obiter dictum: "Civilization is the process of reducing the infinite to the finite." That is the formula for converting romanticism from a discipline of death into a realism that can support a citizenship truly dynamic.

Yearning yields only straining, but creation necessitates actual passage through the bottle-neck of birth with some damage and many a loss, but a loss which must be contemplated manfully as the price not of corruption but of character. Every perfect must be renounced in the name of practice and for the sake of a less perfect made real. This process of diminution becomes exceedingly painful as we approach through the inconvenience of any action at all the extreme discomforts of collective action.

This recession from perfection which discipline both marks and matures may be put almost as a universal law: *there are billions of things that may be felt, millions of things that may be thought, thousands of things that may be said, hundreds of things that may be done, dozens alone of which may be done collectively.*

The climb thus celebrated down the lofty ladder of individual wishfulness to the narrowing exactions of joint endeavor is a recession which informs every life with discipline and scars not a few with cynicism. To avoid the latter and to facilitate our acceptance of the former, let us now clear the path of negatives so that we may advance to the full affirmations of a discipline unequivocally dynamic.

THE NEGATIVES OF DISCIPLINE

The first negative, it is now plain, resides in the very notion of discipline itself. Pure value, the genuinely invaluable, is found in undisciplined but ever fecund fancy. Like all precious ores, it must be mined before it is minted. The second negative resides in the prostitution of the necessity of some discipline to the acceptance of more than is required.

In an ideal world men would, let us presume, have what they want, at least what they need, when they desired it. They would blithely skip the means and happily lay hold upon the ends without further ado. Life would become its own reward, in the very living of it. Prudence would be no virtue in such a world. The universal distinction, however, between means and ends attests how far the world is from such an ideal. Discipline is the child of this discrepancy. Since men want things which they cannot get without a price, they must pay the price or go without. The payment of the price is the simplest and soundest meaning of discipline. What men will pay for ranges all the way from the lowliest sustenance to the loftiest spirituality. When men pay more than what they get is worth, discipline, a natural evil anyhow, becomes now a moral, an unnecessary evil. An unnecessary evil is always disintegrative of some goods. Such discipline is decadent; it dissipates the goods that might be had and it makes brittle to the breaking point the stamina of men by forcing them to ignore the dictates of prudence in a world where prudence is indispensable.

So much for general observations. Let us descend now to the contemporary conflict and consider its mighty negations in terms of discipline. Nazi citizenship, for instance, involves an exorbitant price for an inferior product. The price is abject obedience: theirs not to reason why, theirs but to do and die. The inferior product will bear inspection. At the lowest level and in peace time (if such ugliness and austerity can be called peace), the product purchased was guns rather than butter. In what was perpetrated as peace, German citizens paid a higher price than the product was worth in order later to have to pay a still higher price for a product worth much less, the product of war. That is the very meaning of decadence, the conversion of an evil that is necessary into an evil greater than is necessary. No one can, for example, read Neville Henderson's *Failure of a Mission* without sensing how unnecessary was the war. Munich showed already how much more than the justice to Germany required, how very much more than the justice to Czechoslovakia permitted, could have been achieved short of war, through the compromise system.

Such discipline as constitutes Naziism is a disease; it is a disease, moreover, that is progressive. As freedom thrives on freedom, such discipline not only permits but calls for further discipline until the decay of death ends such living decadence. There is a pathology of the spirit which enjoys what it suffers. When men reach that level the rotten fruit of this discipline is seen in their masochistic enjoyment of it. This disease affects the high and low alike when it becomes a national hysteria.

In Prague, in 1934, at an international gathering of philosophers, I heard a distinguished German representative (it was Nicolai Hartmann) argue that virtues remain virtues whether the times permit their practice or not; and he took courage as the example of a virtue whose integrity need not be dissipated by the fact that the times do not permit its exemplification. Returning through Germany from a debate I had at the same Congress with a Nazi philosopher (it was Willy Hellpach) on the merits of our respective ways of life, I was conversing with a "red cap" in one of the great railway stations in Berlin.

"How are things with you?" I asked, to make talk.

"Fine, just fine," he replied, to make propaganda. "Are you a stranger?" he continued.

"Yes, though I once lived in Germany for some months," I explained, mentioning the year.

"Too bad," he sympathized, "too bad; that was before Hitler."

Without meaning to be rude, I exclaimed, I thought under my breath: "Yes, thank God, that was before Hitler!"

He heard me and quickened his sympathy into reproach: "You don't understand," said he, "you Americans don't ever understand," he continued emphatically.

"Well, what's so good about it?" I asked.

Raising his heavy voice above its phlegmatic bass, he shouted until it ended in a shriek almost hysterical: "Now we have order, Order, ORDER!"

And so he had, so they have—high-tensional like the hysteria which articulates it.

That is the product, *order*, for which Germans and the world have paid so heavy a price. Now order is not without its value. It is one of the goods of man's collective life, a good worth quite a price. But on no free reckoning is it the only good of life, nor even one of the greatest.

In paying a price so heavy for a product so shoddy, Germany has made it impossible, for the time being, for the rest of the world to purchase ends more ideal than order, at any price at all. Degrading discipline to the dregs of utter despotism, she has made it now impossible for others to turn discipline to dynamic ends. That discipline is decadent which fixates upon a small ideal, frustrates large ideals thereby, and in the event makes the small smaller still by the method of achieving it. Only that discipline can rightly be called dynamic which swells through its effectiveness both the quantity and quality of the ideal in action. Boasting her citizenship alone dynamic, Nazi Germany has reduced all ideals to one, has degraded that one in the method of achieving it, and has made it difficult for others to seek other ends or to achieve that single end of order save through imitation of her perverse form of discipline.

Truly dynamic would be the civilization which amplified the ends of life until no ideal is left out, and which then harmonized with the diversity of ends a multiplicity of means existing simultaneously but rendered compatible through specialization. This is the goal that democratic culture has set itself. If we, out of deference to this goal, swell freedom to its utmost, we should have as many ends of life as there are individuals to live it. That would be a resultant both proper and prolific, since free men give each his own interpretation to the business of life. We may without betrayal of that large spirit, however, reduce the ideals of free men to that noble trinity which since Plato has enshrined, even if it has also simplified, our ideals: truth, beauty, goodness—these three; and each of them supreme in its own realm and sphere.

It is of course possible so to conceive each of these ideals as to make them overlap if not make them swallow one another. "Truth is beauty, beauty truth," said Keats; "That's all on earth I know, and all I need to know." No ideal has a monopoly on thus claiming to monopolize other ideals. Note indeed how Horatius Bonar (*Hymns of Faith and Hope*, p. 113) extends the ideal of truth, as Keats did beauty, to practically everything:

>Think truly, and thy thoughts
> Shall the world's famine feed.
>Speak truly, and each word of thine
> Shall be a faithful seed.
>Live truly, and thy life shall be
> A great and noble creed.

Or, turning to John O'Keefe for another example, we find similar license taken with goodness (*Springs of Laurel*, Act II, Scene 1):

> A glass is good and a lass is good,
>   And a pipe to smoke in cold weather;
> The world is good, and the people are good,
>   And we're all good fellows together.

Now these poets but exemplify what all of us do in certain moods. Not only do we obscure our normal categories in the license of living, but we find it delightful to do so in the high gear of friendly converse or at the low level of recuperative slackness. There come times, however, when men must use their terms carefully or pay a price too heavy for slovenliness. Lest we be caught discriminating against our truest friends, the poets, let another of them, the greatest of them, Shakespeare, pronounce for us the required counsel of accuracy:

> Truth needs no colour, with his colour fix'd;
> Beauty no pencil, beauty's truth to lay;
> But best is best, if never intermix'd.
> <div align="right">(<i>Sonnet CI</i>)</div>

In the spirit now of that counsel, let us for a time forego the joys of slackness and for the sake of clarity keep these categories as distinct as we can. The trouble of doing so is modest compared to the pains men pay for augmentation of any one of the great ideals themselves. As Owen Meredith so aptly says (*Lucile*):

Not a truth has to art or science been given,
But hours were ached for it, and souls toil'd and striven.

What I propose as worthy of your co-operation is that we now conceive these three ancient ideals in such manner as by the three to cover all that is uplifted in our culture and yet to prevent their overlapping. In this way, with an economy of concepts, we may achieve coverage of all the ends for which dynamic discipline exists.

Conceiving our spiritual life thus with triune diversity, we should have then to conceive our discipline as threefold. Means can hardly be more simple than their ends. Since truth does not grow wild on trees, the price we pay for it would become the discipline of truth. So for beauty. So for goodness. That price for truth is *science,* for beauty, *art,* for goodness, *politics.* These are the means whereby men keep a new quantity of the diversified ideal streaming, as it were, into our world. Not to keep ideals renewed from age to age is to permit the old to grow stagnant and to pass into its opposite. Any ideal, however precious, without new infiltrations becomes dogma and does to the death the very spirit which it was meant to replenish. James Russell Lowell said:

> Time
> makes ancient good uncouth;
> They must upward still, and onward, who
> would keep abreast of Truth.

To hold the fathers' truth in leash against universal impulses of growth is to "make their truth our falsehood." Beauty without new increments sinks into use and wont and presently ceases to fill eager eyes with luster or prompt any glad heart to skip a single beat. Goodness can so harden when not constantly leavened with new forms of generosity that cruelty is not only tolerated but becomes, as in

Naziism, the standard form of citizenly duty to the group which has the power.

In a happier world we should now proceed at once to demonstrate how these three constructive disciplines—science, art, politics—operate to keep alive the triune values and to swell their collective sum into what we call the spiritual life of mankind. But so unhappy is our world that before turning to our disciplines constructive, we must reluctantly pause to pay our respect to a fourth discipline, the utterly destructive one of war. For, I repeat, by degrading discipline to the decadence of a bogus order the Nazis have drawn the whole world into their sorry train, warping all decent lives athwart the foul pathway of *Führerprinzip*. We will forfeit long future chances at things constructive unless here and now we can excel them at the practice of the deadly discipline of destruction initiated at their insistence. What a burden this lays upon the spirits of free men, to have to do evil that good may possibly be restored!

Let us make clear to ourselves the spirit in which we accept this blighting burden of destructive discipline. Hardly do we fight to make the world better. Probably no war ever made the world any better, and so mankind blames the peace for what peace only terminates. We fight to keep the world from becoming immeasurably worse than it now is. For the whole world to sink as low in spiritual tone as Naziism has sunk would be to lose next to all that civilization has gained. It would be to lose truth to its boasted subversion, a propaganda diabolically intent upon prostituting goodness and beauty no less than truth to the poison of power. It would be to subject beauty to the hazard of minds disordered like Hitler's and Goebbels'. It would be to narrow goodness to racial dominance, and to substitute for equal treatment in the name of justice either servility or arrogance in the name of a "new order." A war which may prevent that otherwise certain result is justified by every counsel of prudence, and would be warranted by even a much slighter probability of success than we at the worst actually have. Death to forestall dishonor is preferable to a life of lies.

To be adult means to know that men must at times choose the lesser evil with the same resoluteness as in happier times they choose the greater good. We have passed through such a time of choice. Not to fight now to a decision is to stand idly by and see the only weapon which the forces of evil understand and respect rust from blood of better men and women already spilt upon it. Let this be the final element to steel our courage for the full acceptance in detail of all that military discipline implies; let this be the plain reminder, I mean, of what Hitler and his satellites are warping us away from to engage with them in the most odious activity known to man, the most odious next to craven acceptance of their intolerance and oppression. Discipline has its "push" as well as its "pull." I have been emphasizing its ideal pull. Let us stop a moment to feel deeply its infamous push in the present situation—and to catch therefrom the full tonicity of counteraction.

This diabolical thing which they have perpetrated has warped us away from both our thought to enjoy the fruits of peace and our will to perfect its processes. It has caused us, reluctantly but at last resolutely, to militarize ourselves into an armed camp of producers and fighters. It has caused us desperately to alter and demonstrably to deteriorate the web of our human relations. We Americans do not normally enjoy suspicion of or circumspection with one another. We have had now, as a result of their perfidious action, to register and fingerprint our aliens, to encarcerate some of them, and to enforce for the first time in our national history, mass migration. We have had to see both Congress and the states tighten in a thousand ways, mostly odious to our sense of tolerance, the bonds between fellow citizens, and to institute continuing investigations of them through federal means and state equivalents.

More intimately than all this, we are driven—and what a negative incentive this gives!—to interrupt all our finest intimacies and to interfere with our most prized procedures. The intimacies of family life, of education, of religion are rudely interrupted to snatch our sons away from comfort and solace to hazards dire and in regions most remote; to postpone or to precipitate the romantic hopes of our daughters; to interrupt and then to disrupt forever the rightful expectations of parents; to decimate educational institutions or to weaken their work with preoccupations adventitious even when not odious; to poison churches with the work and woes of equivocal consciences and their resulting sense of guilt; and to regiment in ways unprecedented our free enterprise by priorities in consumption, interferences in production. All this deterioration of our normal lives is inflicted upon us to constitute for us a colossal push against what violates to the core the integrity of our peace.

Such as this, however, we can stand. We are not sobsisters or sissies; we are not dudes or dandies; we are not wheedlers of fate or whiners for comfort—not we Americans, not yet. Suffering we know to be as much a part of life as is joy, and democracy, we also know, is not privileged to escape its share of the one while enjoying its share of the other. Necessary discomfort we can accept as part of life's normal expectations. Indeed, universal suffering we can accept as the fate of humanity. But wantonly inflicted discomfort, egregiously provoked suffering—these we must accept, when we do accept them, with emotions befitting the deserts of those who inflict them. We accept them in the stern spirit of those late lines from *Punch,* lines to "The German Armies":

> You have gone into a land of no returning,
> Not in the eastern snows nor in the West,
> Made havoc and lit fires that shall be burning,
> Long after the guns rest.
>
> . . . . .
>
> You have gone into a land of no repentance,
> Triumph and trumpet shall not help you now,
> The judge has passed the irrevocable sentence,
> The brand is on your brow.

All that interruption of the will to enjoy we shall accept—accept in the foreboding spirit of that prophetic malevolence. But harder to accept is what we know that acceptance will do to our humane spirits. The damage done to our will to enjoy is as nothing in the long run compared to the impairment of our will to perfect the processes of peace. This will to perfect has lain deeper in us than even the will to enjoy. It had to be so, or else all had been lost; for democracy started with its opposite: it had both to believe in "the perfectibility of mankind" (in order to start from tyranny at all) and to concern itself constantly with improvement (in order to keep from sliding back after it got started). Were the enjoyment of rights and fruits not accompanied by the will to extend to others those rights and to multiply the fruits of freedom, democracy would pass through a lush dotage into a despised death. Deservedly so! For democracy is essentially the will to improve: to improve external conditions so as the better to grow human souls up to the high level of their potentiality. It is the full and deep knowledge that the odious aggressors have deprived us not only of our loves but have filled us with their hates—this is the knowledge dire that constitutes our mightiest push to put them down.

Yet we must not close our negation with mere negatives. Repulsion, which we are justified in having, is for the sake of removing the most odious of objects so that men may modify all malevolence including their own ugly spirit. War with us is for the sake of peace, and this war for the sake of removing such obstacles to peace as will surely minimize war's reappearance. We accept the negative discipline of war not in the romantic hope of ease, but in the realistic determination to resume a way of life disciplined to constructive ends. The push apart, our "pull" is toward the ideal, ever toward the ideal. There abide truth, and beauty, and goodness; and in our keeping are the ways thereunto, science, art, and politics.

As we now unfold these disciplines in order to achieve as well as to disclose these ideal ends, let us remind ourselves of the variety which, under forms of freedom, both bewitch and baffle us. This variety betokens in our case that no one discipline can be recommended with final authority for all citizens. Democracy implies specialization, because it glorifies individual differences. While all values are for all men, they are for all men with differentials. There are three stages, or distances if you will, with reference to value in citizenship, whether the value be truth or beauty or goodness. And there are appropriate distances for different persons with reference to the disciplines of science, art, or politics.

Some citizens will indulge in each. Many more will participate without directly indulging. And, finally, all citizens in a democracy will be beneficiaries of all values. Mass gains must be passed around. We shall trace out in the proper place what this doctrine of discipline means by way of relief from the tension superinduced by a doctrine of moral omni-competence. Many citizens would be miserable as scientists—and failures at science besides. The same with art. And even more than the same with politics. We don't want failures, and constructive disciplines do not imply the kind of suffering that comes from tensions arising from maladjustment of talent to duty.

Citizens do not have to indulge in science, for example, in order to participate in the enterprise; and they do not have even to participate, in order to benefit from a scientific civilization. This is the double democratic doctrine of the dispersion of benefits through the concentration of energies. We shall illustrate this law and clarify it in connection with each separate discipline. So here we need only recommend it as the pull of democratic discipline, and identify it as the main thing which constitutes this discipline, the path which, like the way of the just, shineth more and more toward a dynamic day.

2

Science: The Discipline of Truth

Belief is desecrated when given to unproved and unquestioned statements for the solace and private pleasure of the believer. . . . Whoso would deserve well of his fellows in this matter will guard the purity of his belief with a very fanaticism of jealous care, lest at any time it should rest on an unworthy object, and catch a stain which can never be wiped out. . . . If belief has been accepted on insufficient evidence, the pleasure is a stolen one. . . . It is sinful because it is stolen in defiance of our duty to mankind. That duty is to guard ourselves from such beliefs as from a pestilence which may shortly master our own body and then spread to the rest of the town. . . . It is wrong always, everywhere, and for every one, to believe anything upon insufficient evidence.—W. K. Clifford, "Ethics of Belief."

WITHOUT THE DYNAMICS of truth civilization is both meaningless and impossible. I say meaningless because by civilization we mean a collective life organized in part around the ideal of truth—and certainly devoted to it. But truth must grow in order to survive. To keep it static is to kill it. These two granted, then science can be seen to condition civilization. Science is the means—I shall suggest the *only* means—whereby truth is replenished and civilization thus kept growing.

One does not have to be either a Pilate or a jester to ask the question, "What is Truth?" Necessary to ask, it is fortunately a question which we do not have to answer here. If we did, we should by its difficulty be wholly diverted from our pursuit of the dynamic element in democratic citizenship. We have only to skirt the problem of definition in order to see all that we need to see, to make out our case for science as truth's discipline. Whatever truth is or is not in its innermost essence, there are certain conditions without which we can tell that truth is not present. These conditions yield recognition even though they do not constitute definition. Their absence spells truth's absence, even though their presence may not define the essence of truth.

SCIENCE AS THE STRATEGY OF AGREEMENT

The foremost of these conditions, and the one we shall here emphasize, is agreement of equally able and equally honest seekers after truth. Without some way of effecting this agreement, men are stranded as between conflicting claims. Lo, here is truth. Lo, truth is there. Lo, truth is nowhere dependably! "Truths turn into dogmas the moment they are disputed," says Chesterton. A method which begets voluntary agreement among claimants is the discipline of truth. Such a method science is. But it is a method most difficult to found, hard to support, and disappointing to many in quantity of results. Let us illustrate the matter in reverse.

Suppose those of us who are Methodists in religion had to get the consent of those of us who are Baptists, or the reverse, before we could promulgate our religious beliefs. How much would we proclaim? Some, but less than now. Suppose, further, that we had to beget agreement among all Protestant bodies before we were free to evangelize. Suppose we Protestants had to get the consent of us Catholics, or the reverse, as the condition of propagandizing our beliefs. The body of doctrine would have been by this time sadly cut down, but the task of reduction would have only begun. We would have then to consult the Mohammedans, the Confucians, the Hindus, the Taoists; and coming back home, the Mormons and the Christian Scientists. All these are honest and able people in quest of religious truths. What would remain, after this wide consultation, to be proclaimed as the truth of religion? Something, I hope; but not a great deal.

We have no method in religion for effecting such agreement, and so we preach and accept tolerance for a variety of claims that amounts at times to contradiction. Truth, however, cannot contradict itself. Only that upon which equally honest and able men agree meets the first condition of truth. This is the reason that, apart from a genial looseness of language which I have asked you to renounce, the most knowing men do not now seek to justify the religious enterprise from its relationship to truth. There are other values not less important than truth, and so other justifications; but this *logical* justification is lacking; it would appear *forever* lacking. The best that sectarianism as protestantism (and to aggravate the sectarianism but makes the matter much worse) has been able to achieve in America was stated this year in a great conference called by the Federal Council of the Churches of Christ at Ohio Wesleyan University. Called to lay down specifications for a proper attitude toward the war, and particularly to lay down specifications for the hoped-for peace, the best the conference could achieve regarding the settlement of its own disharmonies was such a statement as led *Time* to say that "they were less drastic when it came to themselves" (than in settling the problems of statesmen). With reference to themselves, they called for "a new era of interdenominational co-operation in which the claims of cooperative effort should be placed, so far as possible, before denominational prestige." That soft phrase "so far as possible" would be ironic indeed if the achievement of truth were the final test by which the value of religion is to be judged. The simple fact is that religion has no method of resolving differences and of begetting agreement. The simple recognition would have saved the stake many a victim and spared many a saint the noose. The simple recognition would have made tolerance the necessary child of one's own self-respect rather than the precarious precipitate of recommended virtue. No, let us put it down as highly important for democratic citizenship that religion has no way of resolving honest differences and of begetting dependable agreement. This constitutes the bed-rock reason for our wise separation of church and state: to divorce religion from the will to power and to free it from every aspect of coercion, to free it for as many forms of the will to perfection as a free people feel. Such purging is religion's only dependable safeguard against provincialism, the provincialism which has led a wit to remark of Unitarianism that it proclaims "the fatherhood of God, the brotherhood of man, and the neighborhood of Boston."

What I say of religion's impotence for truth I say also of my own preoccupation, politics. Suppose that those of us who are Democrats had to convince those of us who are Republicans, or the reverse, that our way of justice is right and theirs wrong before we could proclaim a platform or institute a campaign. Where would we be with reference to political action? We should be where we are with reference to religious conviction, approximately so. For no more in politics than in religion (until we reach the legislative level, and there only through compromise which belies the claim of truth) have we a method of resolving differences and begetting agreement through the parade of evidence. In neither can we "exhaust all adverse hypotheses," the scientific test, as we shall soon see, of the presence of truth. So we justify the discipline of politics, as the practice of religion, in terms of other goods than that of truth.

In science it is, and it would appear in science alone, that we have achieved a method of compounding claims until from initial variety eventual unanimity sometimes results on a world-wide scale. That achievement it is which denotes science the handmaiden of new truth and thereby the savior of old truth from dogma. Our task here is not to demonstrate the details of that method. It is enough for our purpose if we can elicit consent to this claim for science. To further this consent we had best not say, with our opening statement from W. K. Clifford, of *all* belief that "it is desecrated when given to unproved and unquestioned statements for the solace and private pleasure of the believer," but say it, rather, of only the beliefs of scientists about science itself.

It is indeed enough for our purpose to celebrate the finest statement of this ever made and then to illustrate this procedure by the experience of an American scientist. The statement of the philosophy was made by a great French scientist, Pasteur. Louis Pasteur had been at first the butt of many a jibe when he proposed the notion that germs are at the bottom of certain diseases. His contemporaries thought that he was a dreamer who visioned wrongly of things concrete. But men came eventually to think differently, because Pasteur was master of the method which begets agreement among men who are able to observe and honest in report. He led critics to the fountain of observation, and their own honesty in the presence of the evidence compelled them to think as he thought. When the hour of his triumph came, a great institution was erected in Paris bearing his honored name. Peers of science gathered from far and near to do him homage. Pasteur at length arose and put into words of light a philosophy of science which I shall never tire of quoting to illustrate this aspect of democratic discipline:

"This that I ask of you," said he in one pregnant paragraph, "is what you again in your turn demand of the disciples who gather round you; and for the investigator it is the hardest ordeal he can be asked to face—to believe that he has discovered a great scientific truth, to be possessed with a feverish desire to make it known, and yet to impose silence on himself for days, for weeks, sometimes for years, whilst striving to destroy those very conclusions, and only permitting himself to proclaim his discovery when all the adverse hypotheses have been exhausted."

Mark those arduous words: no claim of truth until *"all adverse hypotheses have been exhausted."* That is indeed the great negative that guards the gates of the pure positive value of truth. It is the negative which, lacking, sends religion and politics to other ideal values for justification.

Now let another scientist, this time an American astronomer, Dr. D. W. Morehouse, show us how this discipline of science works in the hands of scrupulous devotees of truth. Dr. Moorehouse left, at his death, notes upon the discovery of the comet that bears his name. As a contribution to citizenship that an enlightened press may make, as well as further to illustrate the caution of scientific discipline, let me quote here entire the account of the matter published by the Des Moines *Tribune* (September 17, 1941):

A third of a century after discovery of the Morehouse comet, the astronomer's own written account of the finding has been made public.

Dr. D. W. Morehouse, late president of Drake University, made the discovery on September 1, 1908.

Recently, Mrs. Morehouse, looking through his papers, came upon his own account, which she said she knew he had written but which had never been published.

Dr. Morehouse was spending the summer of 1908 at Yerkes observatory as a voluntary research assistant under Dr. E. E. Barnard, an authority on celestial photography. In August, Dr. Barnard turned a telescope over to Dr. Morehouse, then 32 years old.

"September 1 was Sunday evening," Dr. Morehouse wrote of his discovery.

"Mrs. Morehouse was quite anxious that I should rest that evening, since I had worked practically every night all summer, but the sky was unusually clear and I insisted that there was a special patch of nebula which I must get that evening.

"I therefore started photographing at the earliest possible moment. About 1:30 or 2 that morning, I stopped the exposure for a few moments. This incident proved valuable in detecting the direction of the comet. I then resumed my work until morning. I had exposed three plates."

Resting then a few hours, according to custom, Dr. Morehouse did not go to the laboratory to develop the photographic plates until midday.

"I developed the larger plate first, and after a casual examination, put it in the drying hood without having detected anything. This plate bore only the tip end of the tail of the comet," his account says.

"I developed the next-sized plate and noticed a strange object on it. I was very familiar with this particular region. I examined the plate in the darkroom while it was still wet, but hearing Dr. Barnard out in the hall, my enthusiasm urged me to take the plate in the washing tray to him which I did.

"Dr. Barnard was not easily approachable when he was busy. I therefore begged his pardon and asked him if he would take a look at this object which I had on my plate. He gave it a glance and said in a rather gruff voice, 'Nothing to it. It is just aberration.'"

Still not satisfied, the young astronomer returned to the darkroom and developed the third plate. Again, he found the strange object in the same position.

"I was then convinced of the nature of the discovery. I took the two dripping plates in my hands and ran upstairs to Dr. Barnard's room, rapped on the door, and Dr. Barnard said, 'Come in.'

"I said, 'Pardon me, Dr. Barnard, but I do have a real object on the two plates.'

"He said, 'Let me look at it.'

"I handed him the two plates; he glanced at them with eagerness. He looked at me, and I looked at him, and we both said with one breath, 'Yes, it is a comet.'

"Then the excitement began."

Before the discovery could be claimed, workers had to be called in from other offices to calculate accurate positions and describe the comet's location at a specific time.

"Dr. Frost, the director, had left the observatory and could not be located," the account continues. "It was an unvarying precedent that the director was to give out all discoveries.

"Dr. Barnard was unwilling to take the responsibility without first finding Dr. Frost. I started out in search of the director. In the meantime, Dr. Barnard became impatient and decided to take the responsibility and send out the telegram.

"The telephone connecting the observatory with the telegraph offic was a rural line. Two ladies were visiting on the line, and Dr. Barnard could not break in.

"Finally, his impatience impelled him to demand the line, saying an important discovery had just been made at the observatory and that he must telegraph the news to Harvard.

"The ladies were very apologetic and gave up the line. By this time, Dr. Frost had been located, and the telegraph wires were ticking out the position of the comet as of September 1, 1908."

That evening, every telescope of the observatory was turned on the comet, and repeated photographs were taken.

"The comet proved to be an enigma from the beginning," the account states. "Its photographic appearance was very bright, but visually it was almost impossible to see."

That same evening, astronomers at the Lick observatory in California and at the Harvard and Metcalf observatories in Massachusetts saw the comet, and after three days "congratulations came pouring in" from Juvesy in France; Heidelberg in Germany; Oxford and Cambridge in England, and several American observatories.

TO TRUTH THROUGH THE DISCIPLINE OF DOUBT

Whoever thinks that truth is a hothouse plant easily matured from any and every sentiment of rationality should take these illustrations to heart. It will be like hugging a stone, but in all serious business it is best to know the worst. "Truth," said George Eliot, "has rough places if we bite it through." We may note, in terms of training, what has to be overcome before men can "impose silence upon themselves for days, for weeks, sometimes for years" and especially what must be overcome before men can "strive to destroy the very conclusions" to which they have so hardly come.

Credence is the normal human trait. From the glad sunrise of childhood to the gentle twilight of dotage man believes any and everything that is told or occurs to him, unless and until adequate reason arises for disbelieving. Not faith but doubt it is that is ever on the defensive. One may demur at the strength of the poet's phrase, "love the lie," but otherwise his thought is impeccable for this believing human world:

> When fiction rises pleasing to the eye,
> Men will believe because they love the lie;
> But truth herself, if clouded with a frown,
> Must have some solemn proof to pass her down.

As against the ancient dogma that he who doubts is damned already, science then puts in self-protection as test of integrity, "He who doubts not is fossilized already." We are most comfortable in believing what other people believe; we are happiest in finding that other people believe what we ourselves believe. An age of joiners is the natural age for men. To dress alike, to talk alike, to think alike, to act together—this is the human standard throughout the whole simian world. "Where known," says George Santayana, "truth is almost always dismissed or disguised, because the aspect of it is hateful."

To resist the ancient undertow of credulity is to grow a mind befitting a scientific age. But it is hard indeed. "Truth is tough," said Oliver Wendell Holmes, the father. "It will not break, like a bubble, at a touch." To pursue it requires resistance to the oldest and most sociable streak in our nature; it involves the acceptance of solitude as a way of life; it requires the cultivation of social distance, the capacity to stand alone. As Oliver Wendell Holmes, the son, phrased it, "No one can cut out new paths in company. He does that alone.... Only when you have worked alone—when you have felt around you a black gulf of solitude more isolating than that which surrounds the dying man, and in hope and in despair have trusted to your own unshaken will—then only will you have achieved." Moreover, the culture of incredulity means the necessity of standing alone empty, so to say. That is the hardest ordeal of all. If a man be full of finality, he can then stand alone with the angels and all the invisible but liveried host of heaven. But to harness one's impetuosity with a disbelief of his own beliefs, until these beliefs are more than beliefs, is to stand awkwardly ambivalent if not downright empty against the suction of the deepest undertow of life. It takes character that has been cultivated to do this. As Emily Dickinson said:

> Assent, and you are sane;
> Demur,—you're straightway dangerous,
> And handled with a chain.

It takes stamina to practice the discipline of doubt. Training is required, training superimposed upon a temperament already predisposed to toughness. Science so conceived is a long story from science as easy symbol of modern prestige. None are so slothful as not to love science conceived as giver of gadgets and begetter of the conveniences of life. This thing which we worship as science has remade our world after one pattern of the heart's desire. It has converted scarcity into abundance. It has mitigated the rigors of northern winters to the balm of southern springs. It is now transmuting the rigors of southern summers into the balm of northern autumns. It has touched necessity with luxury and made luxuries into necessities. It has put the privileges of ancient royalty within the reach of little men. Science as such a servant of mankind is a master which we are all eager to acknowledge—acknowledge without any necessary understanding at all of what science actually is or requires of inner discipline. No one can avoid the beguiling smile of this ever-present goddess. But this has little or nothing to do with the saintliness, albeit secular, of science itself.

There is an austerity, not to say chastity, about science as a hygiene of the inner life which does no injustice to the thought of saintliness. No man enters fully into its sanctuary whom nature has not built along ascetic lines. A man must be able to doubt; he must prefer the salt of want to the stolen sweet of prematurity. Tough-minded boys and girls, encouraged in their toughness of mind from youth up, may become citizen-scientists so that citizens without science may still enjoy the fruits of this way of life. But fruits of science do not fall for the many save as the roots of science are nurtured by the few. The roots of science are the pains of skepticism and the hard responsibility of their containment. These secular saints of our civilized sincerity are children born of imaginative wonder and nurtured on the discipline of doubt.

THE HIGH SELECTIVITY OF SCIENCE

Science is a way of life for which relatively few are fitted temperamentally, and a way of life for which the great majority of men entertain more suspicion than sympathy.

We Americans have never liked the doubters whom we could identify. The identification has been easiest at the religious level. So we made a renegade in peace of the patriot of our first war, the War of Independence. Thomas Paine died in America unwept, unhonored, and unsung. He was even denied the right to vote at his own home (New Rochelle, N. Y.) on the ground that he was not an American citizen. Paine not an American citizen!—he who had done so much to create that citizenship itself. And why denied? Because he had meantime written an honest even if brash book, *The Age of Reason*. The book was itself a religious treatise, undertaken, as Paine proclaimed, to prevent the French Revolution from skidding into atheism and eventual disaster: "lest," as Paine's words run, "in the general wreck of superstition, of false systems of government, and false theology, we lose sight of morality, of humanity, and of the theology that is true." All this, however, made little difference. Paine remained for innumerable Americans, as he became to Theodore Roosevelt, "a dirty little atheist." And this was chiefly because Paine doubted what others believed, even though he himself also believed—what others doubted. It is not enough for spiritual provincialism that men should believe: it is required that men should believe what we believe. That is the poisonous twist credulity always gives to credence; it makes faith sectarian and sectarianism total. No, honest belief is not enough; *our* faith alone will do. Any age dominated by such a mood—and what age is not so dominated for the general?—loves the succulence of science, but not the stringy psychic stuff of which science is made.

What we did to Paine posthumously, we did to Ingersoll while he was still living. Because he doubted what we believed we damned him as a dangerous man, and let his great talents go largely to waste through lack of deep-rooted deference. And in our own time Clarence Darrow, the Paine of modernity and the Ingersoll of humbler eloquence, we made so far as might be into a martyr of "Christian" distrust. Why? Well, he too doubted what we believed, at a level where we could understand his doubting. We do not ourselves doubt and we do not as a people like doubters. We applaud the poetry but not the plain fact of Tennyson's insight,

> There is more truth in honest doubt,
> Believe me, than in half the creeds.

We have hardly as yet arrived at the truth intended by Paine in his declaration that "infidelity does not consist in believing, or in disbelieving; it consists in professing to believe what we do not believe."

I have myself in a short span of two decades seen many examples of this at a level much above that of mere individual concern. I have in this brief period participated in legislative investigations involving the integrity of two universities—one of my own college, the University of Texas, and the University of Chicago during the Wahlgreen investigation. In each case state legislatures, of one of which I was myself a member at the time, spurred on by popular distrust of the skeptical temperament of science, set out to eliminate men the head and front of whose offending was that they were trying to apply to social processes this honest spirit of inquiry. This involves a tentative attitude toward what others regard as settled and a settled attitude toward methods that others regard as dangerous.

At the University of Texas, a man of good character and stable habits was loaded with a charge which in its ambiguity sounded like the charge which when lodged against himself even wise Socrates admitted he could not understand. This professor was charged with (1) being a Socialist, (2) being a Communist, (3) teaching free love, and (4) teaching anti-Christian tenets. I was asked by the chairman whether my professor was a Socialist. I replied that I'd have to know what he meant before I could answer—that socialism meant everything from what a guy believes whom you do not like up to dialectical materialism. He admitted that he did not know what the first term of the charge meant. One after another of the investigating board made like admissions, until at last the accused had to be asked to define the meaning of the accusation! Such ignorance, however, did not mitigate the zeal of persecution.

That turned out happily enough, as did also the Wahlgreen investigation at the University of Chicago. I have only now finished giving some Wahlgreen Foundation lectures at the University of Chicago. This Foundation was established by Mr. Wahlgreen in part as an act of penance, I believe, for the damage he in his ignorance had sought to do the University of Chicago. Though these two cases, and many another one in our history, turned out well, we cannot too confidently affirm with Shakespeare that "all's well that ends well." Every ending is a new beginning, and vigilance here as elsewhere is the price of continued freedom. Defenders of the scientific temper are as necessary at some times as practitioners of it are necessary at all times. America owes Clarence Darrow a debt of gratitude for the service he did science at Dayton, Tennessee, when the legions of credulity were out to make their superstition the legal orthodoxy of a whole fair region of these United States. It takes a skeptic to see the services of the skeptical spirit and to puncture the pomposity of all pretense to science that does not gladly give free way to this essential characteristic.

Where men crave the symbols and welcome the conveniences but distrust the integrity of science, science survives only through moderation of pride and reverence for fact. Let us look with an eye to detail at what this discipline involves. It involves, first, willingness to revise the old upon demand. As Charles Peirce says, "The scientific spirit requires a man to be at all times ready to dump his whole cartload of beliefs the moment experience is against them. The desire to learn forbids him to be perfectly cocksure that he knows already." Shades of Galileo before the metaphysician of Pisa! "Here at Padua," wrote the scientist to his friend Kepler, "is the principal professor of philosophy, whom I have repeatedly and urgently requested to look at the moon and planets through my glass, which he pertinaciously refused to do."

It involves, second, eagerness to present the new. Knowledge itself runs a temperature for communication. It involves, third, self-control enough not to relinquish the old nor to embrace the new until the processes of patience have worked themselves out to an agreement among the competent. Patient skepticism is the *sine qua non* of science. Discovery of this type of mind, deepening of its doubt and maturing of its stamina, subjection of truth-claims to its painful caution, the cautery of cognitive hope by its acids—this is the discipline whereby democracy keeps old truth alive by bringing new truth a-streaming from wonder through experiment to full-bodied facthood. And arduous as a discipline this is!

Now, I do not undertake to say that the survival of democracy depends upon the practice by all of this dire discipline. Indeed, that is where I would depart from the hard counsel of Clifford, with which I have prefaced this chapter. It is *not* wrong "always, everywhere, and for every one, to believe anything upon insufficient evidence." That would be to sidetrack democracy into a monistic pattern like its opposite; it would be to impose a logical totalitarianism upon a life that is infinitely roomier than logic. It would be to go high-tensional in discipline out of deference to a real truth expanded into a veritable superstition, the superstition that truth is the only value which defines civilization. Civilization would be infinitely poorer than it is were this actually so.

This monism of value is a superstition which we need to root out of our lives in order to enter into the kingdom of a mature democratic culture. "The truth," says George Santayana, "is neither our primary good, nor our ultimate good, nor the synthesis of all goods." The stage has been victimized at every epoch of our national development by the hold of this superstition upon our population. Fiction has been hampered and poetry hamstrung in its development. Dramatics in particular have been made distressing symbols of sin, and novels have been read behind barns rather than in the light of free discussion which could have drained their septic quality away. All this because, as the too simple-minded in every age have conceived it: "Everything's either true or false. Fiction is self-evidently not true. Therefore it is false. Therefore this form of the artistic impulse must be harassed when it cannot be abolished." It is out of this type of logical totalitarianism that most of our censorship of art and our distrust of politics have arisen. It is a superstition unworthy of civilized peoples.

Let us not, however, throw out the precious baby of truth with this dirty water of logical ubiquity. It is right and good for most people most of the time to believe many things upon inadequate evidence; else what is to become of gossip, the juice and joy of life? Right for most, this. license is not right for scientists. They are servants of truth, not agents of credulity. It is indeed wrong for scientists as such to believe anything until it has been demonstrated. As specialists they are our devotees to safeguard the gateway to truth. Truth is not all-important, because it is not the only ideal of our culture. It is all-important, however, where it is important, where it is the ideal in question. For a scientist to desert his discipline of doubt is of the order of the treason which it is for a soldier to desert his post of patriotism. It is as sinful as for a saint to desert his discipline of self-denial. As Justice Holmes has said in the quotation which sets the overtone of this whole treatise: "I know of no teachers so powerful and persuasive as the little army of specialists. They carry no banners, they beat no drums; but where they are, men learn that bustle and push are not the equals of quiet genius and serene mastery. They compel others who need their help, or who are enlightened by their teaching, to obedience and respect. They set the examples themselves; for they furnish in the intellectual world a perfect type of the union of democracy with discipline."

Democracy offers us a plurality of values, of which truth is only one; and so democracy exacts of us a variety of disciplines, of which science is only one, the one betrothed to truth. The effort to limit science to a given domain is both ineffective and pernicious. It will roam wherever it will; for there is no domain which may not yield paying dirt for truth, when the painful price has been paid for mining it. Though science cannot be artificially limited to a domain, it is organically limited by the ideal which it serves as means. Worship of truth does not inhibit worship of beauty. Science as a discipline coexists with other disciplines, as its ideal truth coexists with other ideals equally autonomous.

SCIENCE IN THE SERVICE OF CITIZENSHIP

Enough of such analysis. I am not privileged under present auspices to speak of abstract truth as a philosopher would, nor yet of science as a laboratory technician would. I am engaged to speak of science in the service of a citizenship animated by the strategy of truth. How, then, stands science in full relation to our citizenry? Democratic citizenship is dynamic in that it permits a variety of values to coexist and in that it arranges through specialization for the self-renewing growth of the value appropriate to each aspect of discipline. As touching science, the discipline particular to truth, we may say that citizens have three relations to it: (1) *Some citizens indulge in it and enjoy its roots,* (2) *more citizens participate in it and smell its sweet flowers, (3) all citizens are beneficiaries of it and live upon its fruits.*

Citizens Who Indulge in Science

Our first class of citizens in a scientific age are the specialists themselves. They are chosen, when wisely chosen, from youths who are tough-minded and are watched with solicitude through a long educational period. They graduate into an army of the like-minded with a morale all its own. Its members constitute the brave phalanx of which Justice Holmes has eloquently said: "They bow to no one who seeks to impose his authority by foreign aid; they hold that science like courage is never beyond the necessity of proof, but must always be ready to prove itself against all challengers. But to one who has shown himself a master, they pay the proud reverence of men who know what valiant combat means, and who reserve the right to combat against their leader even, if he should waver in the service of Truth, their only queen."

Moreover, though as seen from the outside they are masters merely of one of the means to value, they are also from the inside practitioners of one of the ends of life. Their training has telescoped in their habits the means and the ends until they realize directly the value which they but mediate to others. Few men have more fun than these. There is no *pleasure,* as Bacon observes in his essay upon truth, "no pleasure comparable to the standing upon the vantage ground of truth." A long and arduous climb this discipline is; but, as Nietzsche embittered by a power-drive saw, "in the mountains of truth, you never climb in vain." These disciples of science live in the light of truth and through its effulgence they glimpse all the autonomies of value associated with truth in the enveloping skies of pure ideality. Made lean and healthy through the ascetic strength of skepticism, they find a robust joy in pursuing their ideal end through a disciplined means continuous therewith. They are not martyrs, as appears to outsiders; but masters, as every insider knows. Through their narrowing of the skies, as in every discipline, they detect a brightness that more than compensates them for the breadth that they forego.

As Pasteur says, of the fruits of science, in concluding his austere disclosure of its roots of skepticism: "Yes, that is a difficult task [i.e., the suspension of judgment until "all adverse hypotheses have been exhausted"]. But when, after many trials, you have at length succeeded in dissipating every doubt, the human soul experiences one of the greatest joys of which it is capable."

This inner reward of science when pursued as a way of life, is touched upon with exceeding reticence by men of science. One detects it in their devotion rather than in their utterances. But its social amplitude and its hidden juncture with the more apparent joys associated with action is communicated adequately in Justice Holmes' artistic tribute to the joy of scientific preoccupation, "the secret isolated joy," as he calls it, "of the thinker, who knows that, a hundred years after he is dead and forgotten, men who never heard of him will be moving to the measure of his thought—the subtle rapture of a postponed power." Holmes but asks us to remember that Pasteur marches triumphant with every child who goes to his inoculation against hydrophobia. What sense of power over evil, what joy in prospect for every scientific worker who lifts his eyes to the periphery of his influence! Yes, what looks like martyrdom to truth turns men into masters of value, and leaves them fortified with that largest of all satisfactions, the poignant pleasure of fulfilment of self found in a disciplined devotion to the first of democracy's values, the ideal of truth.

Citizens Who Participate in Science

Hard upon those who indulge in science and who through the penalty of narrowness reap the reward of mastery, come those who merely participate in the progress of science. Prime among these are the educators who recruit from the young and growing those temperamentally fitted to survive the discipline of doubt and to reward the commonwealth for the investment made in their training.

Though easily ignored, this function of recruitment and training is indispensable. This function conditions all other functions. To waste time and money trying to make scientists of those who in the end will not be scientists is high among the things which men ought to mean when they talk of democratic inefficiency (though even such inefficiency is less, I think, in democratic than in totalitarian lands). To remember what science requires and to keep an effective eye out for its peculiar talent from kindergarten to graduate school is for men to participate in science magnificently who are not themselves scientists. Here is scientific reward for parents who thus participate, for teachers who thus participate, for vocational-test makers and intelligence-test givers. All these serve the cause of truth through the discipline of science.

The tough-minded little fellow who does not believe what

the teacher tells him and who keeps on not believing it, even though perchance forbidden to say so, is a candidate for the further systematic discipline of doubt which science enshrines and ennobles. The participation of educators in science is enhanced if they add to the job of recruiting this temperament the clairvoyance in its training which deepens doubt and fortifies its bearer with the patience to stick out the test set for scientific stamina by Pasteur's injunction.

This is a contribution indispensable for science, as science is indispensable for the career of democracy. They also serve with equal honor who as politicians safeguard the sanctity of science from attacks by those who most deeply distrust its discipline of doubt. To discourage intermeddling in the management of scientific institutions by those who would but be excited to suicide by what they find, is a large and positive participation in science. It is not confined to political servants, but they have frequent chance at such high service. The politicians who appropriate funds match in public life those in private business who support pure research beyond the vision of financial returns. Public funds are so competed for everywhere and at all times that that portion which goes into research reflects credit upon the judgment of all who withstand more immediate pressures. Our national faith in education and tolerance of research has given us, in each generation to date, sufficient public servants who have participated in science with the courage here described.

Perhaps enough has now been said to indicate how meaningful and worthy of honor is this second dimension in the service of science.

All Citizens Benefit from Science

Let us begin the discussion of our third dimension of the influence of science in citizenship by crediting those with some service to science who only tolerate the existence of a spirit so alien to their own. This tolerance in no sense militates against the benefits they receive from science in ways tangible, but it makes them beneficiaries also in ways intangible and indirect. By tolerating skepticism they postpone the finality of fanaticism in their own lives. This minimum spiritual benefit bequeathed by science is swollen toward the maximum for those whose participation in its spirit is more direct and hearty. To debunk human presumption from making divine claims is to give all men the benefit of a light that shines at the heart of civilization; for civilization is the tolerance of variety until we can learn to prize the plurality of value for its own sake.

This prizing of pluralism is not only the first condition of our passing from truth to the other equally precious values, but it is also the last condition of the citizenly enjoyment of the life of values for which democracy exists. Let us celebrate this spirit of growth in the moral of a simple "Bird Song" by some unknown poet:

> I first lived in a little house and lived there very well.
> I thought the world was small and round and made of pale blue shell.
>
> I next lived in a little nest, nor needed any other:
> I thought the world was made of straw and brooded to my mother.
>
> One day I flew beyond the nest to see what I could find.
> I said, "The world is made of leaves; I have been very blind!"

At last I flew beyond the tree, quite fit for grown-up labors.
I don't know how the world is made—and neither do my neighbors.

To have entered into this kingdom of the growing through the discovery, with Holmes, that at no stage are we God, is to secure not only the joy in growth but to safeguard ourselves against the presumption of any *Führer* who has not himself discovered the conceit in his presumption of omniscience.

This joy in growth is, however, vague and perhaps even thin for most men as compared to the thick and concrete benefits which science lays at the door of every civilized man. The patrician of Periclean democracy who owned a dozen slaves had little up on the average American citizen with the Aladdin of science at his beck and call. How shall we adequately celebrate the million ways in which science renders us all beneficiaries of its knowledge applied to life? The milk bottle upon our back step when we awake but ushers in a day ushered out with the last sleepy flick of our reading lamp, a day nurtured, matured and ended in the beneficent orbit of science. The purity of our water, the colors and durability of our clothes, the comfort of our skins, the enhanced flow of our gastric juices—all these stand in relation of beneficiary to benefit as touching the role of science in our lives.

As the spirit of healing and comfort has passed from body to mind, we begin, through psychiatry, the banishing of superstitions in order to lift the ceiling of sanity upon the thoughts of tens of thousands of suffering men and women. There is no realm of life into which the spirit of inquiry does not at times enter, and there are many realms into which it has come for lasting tenancy. As we move from the triumph of ever more and more sound bodies to the creation of minds more and more sane, we but write through the strides of science in the service of truth the sacred pean of praise for the inquiring spirit. "You shall know the truth and the truth shall make you free." The straightening of every crooked path is the summary of the service of science as man walks by faith in truth into his venture with the future.

We join at this level of universal benefits from science the poet's pean of praise for science and its beneficences to our age:

> On the small circle of this ancient stage
> In stranger roles than Homer ever dreamt,
> I enter now—a smooth, titanic age—
> This scene against all prompters to preempt.
> All things are known or probed by me: I train
> Impartial vision on gigantic suns,
> On mites in grass, or in my living brain
> Upon the very stuff where knowledge runs.
> Thus I—this moment lent the flesh and bones
> Of those before me, or those whispering yet
> In the wings of the future—take my cue in tones
> The constellations shall not soon forget;
> And though lights flicker fast, and exits slam,
> Give to the galleries: I AM THAT I AM.
> —Robert Wolf.

This is the discipline of science in full service to democratic citizenship.

3

Art: The Discipline of Beauty

I dwell in Possibility
A fairer house than Prose,
More numerous of windows,
Superior of doors.

Of chambers, as the cedars—
Impregnable of eye;
And for an everlasting roof
The gables of the sky.

Of visitors—the fairest—
For occupation—this—
The spreading wide my narrow hands
To gather Paradise.
                    —Emily Dickinson

THE DEMOCRATIC way of life exists to serve and to be served by the ideal of beauty. No less by beauty than by truth—no less, no more. It is another example of the leeway of democratic liberty, that not one of our trinity of ideals can be presumptuously reared into permanent precedence. All three ideals are indispensable and so equally autonomous. All are valuable, each invaluable; and so they are not subject to invidious comparison. Some men may happily specialize in service of one of them; some in service of another of them; some periods may profitably give precedence to one, some to another.

Each servant of the ideal will with gentle prowess try from time to time no doubt to promote the form of it which he serves to include all other forms of the ideal. The logical-minded will talk, for instance, of the truth of art and religion, as well as of the truth of science. This is his way of insinuating what he serves into superiority. The artist will spread the mantle of beauty over everything from a syllogism demonstrating the existence of God on up, or down, to the scientific precision of a surgeon's knife—

"it was a beautiful operation!"—as well as over the products of the disciplined arts. And the servant of goodness will in wistful mood make these lines of Emily Dickinson the joint moral of both truth's and beauty's prides:

> I died for beauty, but was scarce
> Adjusted in the tomb,
> When one who died for truth was lain
> In an adjoining room.
>
> He questioned softly why I failed?
> "For beauty," I replied.
> "And I for truth,—the two are one;
> We brethren are," he said.
>
> And so, as kinsmen met a night,
> We talked between the rooms,
> Until the moss had reached our lips,
> And covered up our names.

The moralist, that is, will see truth to be a good and beauty to be a good. What he himself serves will then become *the* good, triumphant over both of them when,

> The moss has reached their lips,
> And covered up their names.

All such preoccupational vanity is natural, and not unwholesome, if pursued in a climate of option that is genuinely tolerant. In such an atmosphere no citizen need be humiliated by professional prowess, and no ideal is in any sense eliminated by such assumed priority. All the ideals are necessary all the time, and the over-will to have it so constitutes the rich stamina of our way of liberty— this being its distinguishing characteristic and a final form of its justification.

Little more often than truth, however, does beauty grow wild on trees, to be plucked at will by the easygoing. Such beauty as is free is also fleeting, making itself thin pleasure into which it vanishes, or turning into its opposite through insensitive familiarity. Beauty, like truth, requires discipline to bring it to birth and to keep it growing. "All things excellent," to quote Spinoza (a second time), "are as difficult as they are rare." Beauty has many forms and its diverse excellencies glint through many different apertures of man's enflamed sensitivity.

All these, however, through that oversimplification which discussion requires, we now imprison under the single discipline of art. The arts themselves are many, but they are also one on the leeward side in that they are all agents of the ideal called beauty. Art is no shortcut, but the long, hard, excellent way from where men are born to where they go if life is to achieve its major excellence. This is far from being fully grasped by the general, especially far from being grasped in the form of art known as fiction. "What is not generally understood," says Sherwood Anderson, "is that to do violence, to sell out a character in the imaginative world, is as much a crime as to sell people out in the real world."

ART DISTINGUISHED FROM SCIENCE AS DISCIPLINE

No less taxing on energy and ambition than the discipline of truth, our discipline of beauty is, nevertheless, not the same as that of truth. The discipline of beauty is indeed of as nearly the opposite quality from the discipline of truth as may be found. To make this difference clear is to serve both truth and beauty, for it is to enlist in the service of each those most fitted to that service while enhancing at the same time the tolerance and gratitude which each must feel for the other in a healthy polity.

Science, as we have seen, requires skepticism to resist ceaselessly the deepest undertow of human nature, the impulse to believe without evidence what can for truth's sake be believed only upon adequate evidence. This discipline of doubt is difficult and even dangerous unless attended by compensations for its narrowness which we are now to find in art. Its difficulty we have sufficiently emphasized, but its dangers not yet adequately. All discipline is indeed dangerous, as we shall not too often remark, when the discipline gets divorced from the idea which marks and ends its usefulness. Any discipline made an end in itself—and every discipline has a certain tendency in that direction—impoverishes life. Of this particular pathology of the spirit let us be forever informed.

There is, however, another danger attending upon the discipline of science which we must make very clear in order to clarify at the same time the nature of the discipline artistic. Science is a narrowing and a cramping thing when taken without its compensations. Skepticism itself is a contracting of imaginative energies to a level far below the full capacity of imagination. Who has not seen the man whose impoverishment but echoes the warning pronounced by Pope against the individual who, born for the universe, narrows his mind and to this or that discipline gives up what was meant for mankind?

Out of the total field of fancy, for instance, science narrows interest at the very beginning to "suggestions" that are or may be made into "hypotheses." Only that relatively small segment of the imaginative life which offers something to be proved, demonstrated, is relevant to truth or is of concern to science. Now this fact itself constitutes initially a mighty falling off from fancy. Santayana has described this domain, and truly described it, as "the tragic realm of truth." Its narrowness is attested by the small number of things which science is able to establish beyond peradventure. With eyes full upon this fact, I have been led in another connection to venture some such overvaluation of the scientific way of life as this: perhaps the best that can be expected from it are (1) more and more gadgets for the comfort and convenience of mankind; (2) a precious substitute on the part of a few active research-workers of a joy in the pursuit for mankind's coveted joy in the possession of truth; and (3) a spreading to more and more sensitive men, like Unamuno, in an age emphasizing science without its compensations, of the tragic sense of life. Perhaps the best indeed that can be said for science in the context of the high hope which it has raised is *that it has made and will make major contributions to only one of the several needs of the human spirit.* This strange tragic note is almost indigenous to the career of science, which is to say to any single-minded devotion to the value of truth. Who has better voiced it than Jamie Sexton Holme?—

> I have been a pilgrim
> On a long quest.
> I have gone from hearth to hearth,
> Passed from breast to breast,
> Thinking to find the answer,
> Hoping for rest.

> I have wandered endlessly
> Round the world's girth,
> Seeking ease for a mind
> Haunted from birth
> By all the torturing
> Dark things of earth.
>
> I have worshipped strange gods
> Of earth, air, and sea,
> Offered many a sacrifice,
> Made many a plea,
> Only to find there is no answer,
> And no rest for me.

I do not wish to overplay this limitation of science, this inadequacy of truth as the exclusive motivation for life. Scientists also serve mightily who but exploit their own limitations. Where truth is the theme, truth, as I have earlier argued, is all-important; and where truth is thus important, science is indispensable. What I here have wished to add is that a tremendous personal price is paid for the truth achieved through science. That major price is the narrowing of the wide human spirit to a single focus in the marvelously roomy galaxies of imagination.

In contrast with art no one has, I believe, put this narrowness of scientific discipline better than did Darwin—both the fact of the narrowness and the bitter personal cost of the fact. Speaking in his autobiographical sketch of an early love he had for poetry, he continues: "I have also said that formerly pictures gave me considerable, and music very great delight." And then he adds: "But now for many years I cannot endure to read a line of poetry: I have tried lately to read Shakespeare, and found it so intolerably dull that it nauseates me. I have also almost lost my taste for pictures or music...." At length he concludes the story of his atrophy: "My mind seems to have become a kind of machine for grinding out general laws out of large collections of facts, but why this should have caused the atrophy of that part of the brain alone, on which the higher tastes depend, I cannot conceive."

It is doubtful whether the deprecation which this loss led Darwin to make of himself was comparatively justified, and even doubtful whether he could have prevented the loss, as he suggests, by a more continuous taking thought of poetry and music during his years of intense scientific preoccupation. There is a certain price which men must pay for their virtues. Darwin had elected the service of truth, and the price paid for that dedication is, more largely than he recognized, an inevitable thing. Personally tragic as was his loss, who will dare say in the light of his magnificent work for science that his sacrifice was not immeasurably worth while for mankind? Servants of truth dare not expect success without sacrifice.

All this I have said not to depreciate science, nor to deny to truth its rightful devotion; but to introduce art as corollary to science, and beauty as compensation for truth in the fulness of democratic citizenship. After saving what he can for himself of imaginative breadth, the scientist saves for mankind the full reach of ideal value by acknowledging beauty as equal with truth and by revering the work of the artist as he expects deference for his equally indispensable work. These words upon the nature of scientific discipline enable us to state now by contrast what is the function as well as the nature of the discipline artistic. The upshot of artistic service is to stretch the human soul.

Science contracts the life of imagination below its normal functioning, down to hypotheses. Art expands the life of the spirit beyond its normal limits, up to acceptance of all which the mind's eye can discern. Stretching is as painful as contracting—and no less fruitful in its results on and for citizenship.

When we can catch artists young and expand their impulses of citizenship in this upper direction, we are serving the democratic enterprise as fully as by catching scientists young and contracting their energies to the service of truth. In science we are after the tough-minded young skeptics, to make them into systematic doubters and probers, thus swelling the sum of truth. In art we are after another type, the feel-ers and the see-ers. We want citizens sensitive-minded. We want them as early as possible: those who see more, hear more, feel more than most. We seek such as can stretch their souls with sufferance and live to tell the tale for all it's worth: to tell the tale in sound or color or form or rhythm. We want souls who in advance of esoteric salvation have already "tasted the bliss of every heaven and felt the pangs of every hell." For to look where others look and see what they do not see; to attend to what others listen to and hear what they do not hear; to touch what others suffer, and quiver to what they hardly even suspect—this is to become "God's spy," an artist eavesdropping, with Emerson, upon a "dialogue divine":

> And the poet who overhears
> Some random word they say
> Is the fated man of men
> Whom the ages must obey.

ART: THE DISCIPLINE OF BEAUTY 59

The developing of man's imaginative capacity to the very top of clairvoyance, this is another indispensable aspect of the business of democratic citizenship.

THE DISCIPLINE OF STRETCHING

Let us first make as clear as may be from the outside, then expand from the inside, the exact nature of this discipline which constitutes access to our fount of beauty. As the skepticism of science contracts the souls of men to or toward the demonstrable as goal, so the contemplation of art expands imagination to or toward the communicable as its own fulfilment. If in developing this thesis, I fall back predominantly upon the poets, it is both because I personally know this form of beauty better than other forms of art and because philosophically I suppose poetry to communicate more to more people than other equally honorable embodiments of beauty. With Emily Dickinson,

> I reckon, when I count at all,
> First Poets—then the Sun—
> Then Summer—then the Heaven of God—
> And then the list is done.
> But looking back—the first so seems
> To comprehend the whole—
> The others look a needless show,
> So I write Poets—All.

Discussing such high matters once with a selected group of students, and speaking in the context of the truth motif, I challenged them to lift their eyes toward the hills of beauty, indeed I prodded them.

"You are dumb," blustered I, "dumb in the presence of immortal beauty. Even if you were to see what God has given us to see, you could not communicate it; for you have neglected mastery of the only means through which adequate verbal expression comes. You no longer study the poets, the poets who alone exploit language to the full and so enable us to celebrate together the single touch of nature that makes all mankind most akin. Failing at the technique of communication, you lack the unearned but final increment of meaning which comes back from the sparkling eye, the tender smile, and the caught breath of another. That deference to expressed beauty, that it is," I continued, "which is the deepest stimulus to the further discipline owed by every man to beauty."

Seeing that I had the attention of all, and was arousing the antipathy of some, I grew more specific.

"Yes," said I, "you are the symbols of neglected talents. You are in this deeper sense the 'lost' generation. You tear your voices to tatters in a gregarious spurge at the games, but you know not the ecstasy of solitude, the elegance of intimate communication, the fertilizing touch of a reciprocally responding soul."

Observing a girl on the front row shaking her head violently in disagreement, I continued, glancing frequently at her, "Yes, you are the victims of spiritual poverty; partly of our culture, but fatally of yourselves." Then I made bold to grow quite specific: "It is next to certain that not one of you can put into genuinely communicable language ten per cent of the experiences you yourself regard as significant." Addressing myself now to the most dissenting member, I said to the girl on the front row:

"You don't believe what I'm saying?"

"I don't believe a word of it, Sir," she replied.

"Why, you yourself cannot put into words," ventured I, "the simple experience of—of—." I was trying, you see, for some illustration that would bowl her over. Failing to get what I thought the right example, I said to her:

"Do you like pumpkin pie?"

"I'm crazy about pumpkin pie," she replied in the vernacular of the period.

"Well," hazarded I, "you can't put into words the simple experience, then, of eating pumpkin pie!"

"Will you give me until tomorrow?" she asked.

"Take as long as you need," replied I.

The next day she gave me these lines, mixing my own bravado and her adolescent breeziness with real feeling for the subject,

> With a warmth like a father's love,
> Spiced as an Irish pun,
> Soft as the purling summer stream,
> Rich as the melting sun,
> Like liquid velvet glide,
> And mid my vitals lie—
> Oh, glad were I to perish
> While eating pumpkin pie!

Her line, "Like liquid velvet glide," illustrates at a rather high adolescent level, I think, what A. E. Housman has described as the "secretion" of beauty—and indeed what a great philosopher, himself no mean artist, has described as one aspect of the discipline of art. I refer to Mr. George Santayana.

Stripping art of all its "artiness," this philosopher puts this, our second democratic discipline, at its simplest and purest when he conceives it—"pure intuition of essence" apart—as "nothing but manual knack and professional tradition." The belittling tone of his "nothing but" is explained by that upon which the emphasis is here put, imaginative expansion. If you rule out of art what it is actually about, then you can of course describe what remains with a certain ironic condescension. Santayana does not despise "manual knack" nor yet "professional tradition." They each have a role in bringing beauty to concrete birth, but it is the role of readying the agent, of steadying the midwife, not the role of creating the subject, beauty, which is to be delivered.

On the external side, both personal and social, the discipline of art is, however, more like science than my sustained contrast would suggest. The artist must master his medium: he must become dextrous, whatever the form of his art. He will do well also to join the scientist in keeping touch with his fellow-workers—"professional tradition"—in the creative life. There is no substitute for the opportune sharing of experience: it trims away excesses, it keeps one toward the center of the stream or at least aware of both the banks, and it fortifies the spirit with morale, at times with inspiration. These are all important; they are a part of the discipline of beauty; but they are important more or less externally.

Internally, what is important is what Santayana excludes from his formal depreciation. It is what he calls "the intuition of essence." This is the inner life of art; this is the veritable approach to beauty. The discipline of soul which makes intuition itself possible is the spiritual price paid for laying hold through imagination upon the pure stuff of fancy. It was this which my student had approached in the line, "Like liquid velvet glide." That line reflects discernment of the psychic precipitate which turns the mere act of eating into an art and climaxes sensuous pleasures with aesthetic clairvoyance. To isolate, to celebrate, to communicate the resulting precipitate, that it is to do the work of the artist in the full service of beauty. My student achieved at her own level the communication of the essence of the pleasure in question. Her best line so nearly catches and releases to another the quintessence of that delightful feeling as pulverized pumpkin goes over the palate's top that more than once when I have wanted, but lacked, the pie, I have half satisfied myself by softly substituting therefor her laryngeal liquidity.

Adolescence apart, however, Mr. George Santayana has described the technique of intuition as "the trick of arresting the immediate." Whoever has mastered this trick can lay hold upon beauty. What is caught through this act may even be the scientist's truth, but if so it will be now not what is demonstrated or is demonstrable; it will be what needs no demonstration at all. It is there, existing in its own right and awaiting only the discipline which can break through the shell of wont to discover it. The children of fancy, like Charles Lamb's "dream children," are all fair, if we take them for what they are and not another thing. The scientific effort to prove them true is to obfuscate intuition of essence with extraneous questions and qualities. They are what they are in their own right, and for an artist to become a good shepherd of his own thoughts, in the sense that he can enter upon his find, is for him to have disciplined himself into the ways and wonders of beauty.

Only the disciplined, however, can fully "secrete" this distillate of discipline. Those who would have the honey without becoming workers in the hives are but aesthetic drones. Dryden has described them:

> Damned Neuters in their
> Middle way of steering,
> Are neither Fish, nor Flesh, nor
> Good Red Herring.

This discipline, I repeat, consists primarily of a stretching of the soul, not only beyond preoccupation with truth but—and this is even harder—beyond preoccupation with morality as well. Goodness is a great ideal, and we shall presently present it as such. But its greatness is not rightly usurpative, and to apply its authority beyond its jurisdiction is to impoverish democracy with a kind of totalitarianism other than the logical one which comes from making truth supreme. Santayana has been at some pains not to depreciate either truth or goodness, but to enhance, nevertheless, the third of our autonomous ideals, that of beauty.

The spiritual life—and that's what democratic citizenship is finally about—arises from cultivation of the total life of imagination, nothing less. "It is only in contemplative moments," says Santayana, "that life is truly vital." The only attitude that safely conducts us to value's entirety is therefore one of "disintoxication" from this or that value. All that belongs to a quiet eye constitutes the soul's legacy and its legitimate harvest. It is this supreme treasure of imaginative totality which Santayana early discovered. As against his parents and teachers, who with one voice told him that religion, for instance, is a work of imagination and therefore is bad, Santayana says that he learned to respect their observation while rejecting their conclusion. From childhood he discerned, as he puts it, that "the works of human imagination are good, they alone are good; and the rest—the whole real world—is ashes in the mouth." Morality with its depreciations, no less than science with its discriminations, can become deadly influences, both, in the full career of value. Beauty, like truth and goodness, has its own discipline and through that discipline distributes its blessings to civilization.

EMILY DICKINSON UPON THE DOUBLE DISCIPLINE OF BEAUTY

We have now to illustrate both aspects of beauty's discipline—intuition of essence and technical dexterity—with an artist whose stature is not less than that of Pasteur in science. Emily Dickinson has written the proper prescription for this discipline, proper in general and fruitful in particular. Contemplating her breath-taking clairvoyance and her uncanny strategy of communication, one can almost allow her the license of her poetic claim,

> I found the phrase to every thought
> I ever had but one. . . .

In general, says she:

> To make a prairie it takes a clover and one bee,—
> And revery.
> The revery alone will do
> If bees are few.

Detailing now this general truth, she gives, will one but see it so, this description of what it takes to be an artist:

> The soul selects her own society,
> Then shuts the door;
> On her divine majority
> Obtrude no more.

> Unmoved, she notes the chariot's pausing
> At her low gate;
> Unmoved, an emperor is kneeling
> Upon her mat.
>
> I've known her from an ample nation
> Choose one;
> Then close the valves of her attention
> Like stone.

If it be not sacrilege, let us with logical license expand her poetic clairvoyance. In the first stanza our artistic guide is telling us that solitude is essential to the creative life, no less in art than in science. She reminds us with another clairvoyant soul—Justice Oliver Wendell Holmes, whom we have already cited—that "No one can cut out new paths in company. He does that alone."

This is a reminder desperately needed by citizenship in a collective-minded age. It constitutes only the down payment, itself which few can make, upon the soul's finest investment. A woman fully grown and educated at the university confided in me of late, as her phrase went, that she was "a complete wreck" when she had "to spend an evening alone." Against that typical-sounding reaction of our time, when the "psyche" has so often in fact as in pragmatic theory become a "socius," place for sanity's dear sake Dickinson's wiser insight, that wherever the soul stands alone, selecting her own society, there stand with her "her divine majority."

We carry within ourselves, and nowhere else, the capacity not only to remake the earth through the power of hypothesis proved true, but also to present the ideal to contemplation as a form of perfection awaiting mortal embodiment through the discipline of art. As James Russell Lowell said, in remarking the contribution to universal citizenship of the genius of Robert Burns,

> We find within these souls of ours,
>   Some wild germs of a higher birth,
> Which in the poet's tropic heart bear flowers
>   Whose fragrance fills the earth.
>
> . . . . . .
>
> All that hath been majestical
>   In life or death since time began,
> Is native in the simple heart of all,
>   The angel heart of man.

It is this world within the world to which disciplined minds shut themselves in when they shut the world itself out. Dickinson's second stanza reports one episode out of billions which fancy may fulfill. Solitary within her own house and garden, supported by her own iron will, probably a lonely object of pity for most, she was wooed unmoved and so left unwon by royalty pausing uninvited at "her low gate." What others strive for unavailingly in the world of society was hers without the asking when she stayed in a room lighted by the light which never shines on land or sea. Whoever is at home whenever the soul calls on herself, he will be called upon by a thousand attendants liveried in the world's most prideful purple. To secure all this you need only solitude in which to practice "the trick of arresting the immediate." So practiced a fisherman as Emily Dickinson could hardly let her net down a single time without drawing up at least one bowing prince charming. Moreover, his perfection as ideal would be more real than the virtues of any actual prince of flesh and blood.

All this Emily Dickinson is saying, or seems to be saying, for art, whatever else she may have been saying in particular to her own wounded and fugitive heart.

Then in the last stanza of the poem before us, she touches, or seems to touch, upon the discipline required as technique if the cloudland of fancy is to precipitate itself in the gentle dew of achievement. Out of the skies of fleeting images, the soul must choose "one" and then adamantly preoccupy herself with it until it is surely born for others to see and enjoy. It is never a full citizenly act for sensitive souls merely to contemplate in solitude the marvels of imagination. True, it requires discipline to do so, a discipline infinitely rewarding to the inner life of man, a discipline without which little else can be made rewarding to man. But it requires a discipline which adds to concentration the finest craftsmanship to bring imaginary beauty to collective birth. The mind must "close the valves of her attention like stone" while she wreaks her vision against recalcitrant materials until they yield access and residence to her insistent insight.

That completes the double aspect of artistic discipline: the power, first, to arrest the immediate and to behold it in all its essential majesty and then, second, the stamina and skill to clothe the chosen perfection with the garments of finitude without marring beyond repair its eternal essence. Whoever can do this double duty is fully disciplined to shoot the ugly realities of life through and through with some living semblance of the ideal. To such a one, the voyage of life may become in its better stretches a journey,

> Where ships of purple gently toss
> On seas of daffodil.

ART IN THE SERVICE OF CITIZENSHIP

Art, like science, is, however, a large subject—much larger than I have as yet made it appear. As touching art, the discipline particular to beauty, we may say, as we have said of science, that citizens have three relations to it: (1) *Some citizens indulge in art and enjoy its roots*, (2) *more citizens participate in it and smell its sweet flowers*, (3) *all citizens are beneficiaries of it and live upon its fruits.*

Citizens Who Indulge in Art

It is the first class of citizens, those who indulge in art, of whom I have been thus far primarily speaking. Artists are the men and women who have caught a vision of beauty and have mastered a technique for its communication. "Most people are afraid to trust their imaginations," says Sherwood Anderson, "and the artist is not." His discipline is of the body's eye or hand or ear, as well as the larger trust of the mind's eye. His reward is, across the gulf in others separating mind and body, to unify the mental and the physical until each man participating in his achievement functions as a single living soul.

This is an achievement second to none in importance. Most men carry divided selves. The will to power which connects us with the animal order fills us with energy and drives us hither and yon through the impetus of action. The quieter will to perfection which lies in many men sleeping, though in none wholly dead, would stay the drive until some work is done worthy of aspiration's deepest being. Looking, as God looked, upon something which represents our best, we now and then say, with Him, "Behold, it is good." Continued care for these rare and precious starvelings, arising in the interstices of our haste, would nurse in us a solicitude, almost maternal, to leave no dream unbodied and to shed nothing from hands or loins ungirt with love. To function for one whole day up to the level of all our powers, harnessed at last in the perfect drive of a single high purpose—this would be to live at last.

Such joys those know, and almost they alone, who have become artists in fact. It is human for a scientist to look, with Pasteur, upon the positive results of his skepticism and call it true. It is hardly short of divine for the artist to survey the ideal embodied, and truly name it beautiful. Though I have quoted it elsewhere, I do not too much apologize for quoting here again the all but perfect expression of this artistic fulfilment throughout the wide reaches of the fine arts entire. The lines are Jamie Sexton Holme's:

> If I might seize and capture in a song
> One cadence that would ever charm the ear—
> One burst of melody as sure and strong
> As from the larks at summer dawn I hear—
> If in a poem I might crystallize
> One flying gleam of passion's swift surprise,
>   Or in the ageless permanence of stone
> Prison some gesture's fugitive loveliness—
> If I might paint that shining golden tress
> The wandering wind across your eyes has blown—
>   Oh, if in some way I could make my own
> One fleeting and uncapturable thing,
> So men would come and hear, or see, or sing,
> Saying the while of me—perhaps long dead—
>   "Oh Beauty! here wast thou interpreted—
> Here spoke thy slave, here toiled thy votary!"—
> I should lie quiet in my narrow bed,
>   And ask no more of immortality!

Such is the deep reward—the reward of having so lived while life afforded that they do not have to demand to live when life is done—of those fortunate devotees of beauty who have disciplined themselves for its dear sake. But the contribution of art to citizenship does not stop with those who directly indulge. To them alone is given the grace to say with Sherwood Anderson, if all would say it: "If the power were to be given me to change the whole social structure of life by turning over my hand I would not dare to turn it over." Contentment with the contemplative is not, however, the whole lot of men in a world as evil as it is good. The will to power moves too deeply for most men to permit what of evil they might efface. As in science, so here: there are many more who participate than indulge in the career of beauty.

Those Who Participate in Beauty

And chief among these participants in the cause of beauty are those who recruit and train sensitive subjects to become the artists who in turn indulge in the career of that discipline. Parents serve beauty who are wise to the inclinations of children, who furnish them with clay, who sensitize them to sound or color, who whet their curiosity for many a fugitive access to beauty's domain. The teachers also serve who, out of the multitude that pass their doors, keep keen eyes for those who may with care become creative in imagination. And following upon this general selective care of parents and teachers, come those who serve the arts as special trainers in the several dexterities which lay foundation for appreciation, even when the final result is not actual discoveries of new forms of beauty.

Custodians of art treasures, exhibitors and distributors of art products, improvers of industrial designs, managers of men in aesthetic collectives like the cinema, these and such as these are not without wide significance in the total enterprise of beauty. Patrons of art, though themselves not artists, participate helpfully in the business of recommending beauty to men. Robbed of its patrons, art would be largely reduced in any age to the esoteric community of those few who do but indulge in the creative life. All entrepeneurs of art also serve the precious enterprise of imaginative enhancement.

The Whole Community as Beneficiaries of Beauty

At last we come, in art as in science, to the universal spread of the ideal. Loose the influence of beauty in the world and no living human being is wholly alien to its affluence. Take all song out of life, and consider what then would be missing from the joy of ordinary living. Remove all color save what comes free, and consider what more is gone from life. Remove all dancing and dramatics and with them every form not spontaneously arisen in nature; and, with all these gone, inquire how much of the meaning of life would be left. "Beauty," we cannot but reiterate with Plato, "is a smooth slippery thing which easily slips in and dominates the soul."

There is frequent complaint that art has become more and more a thing of passive enjoyment, something brought to us while we are sitting down, relaxed if not listless. There would be much aesthetic improvement, no doubt, were every citizen himself a creator in some sphere of art, however small the sphere. But what art adds to life even when art is vicarious is hardly short of enormous. It is easy to misjudge a spectator. The word "listless" does not well evaluate the benefit many mere listeners get from music, and I should want to rate even higher the ecstasy that comes to some from the melodious rendering of a poem written by another than either the reader or the hearers.

Instead of grief for what is lost through large-scale production, which means also, as it were, absentee consumption, there is every reason to be grateful for what is gained when the influence of art is spread wide, even though it may appear thin to those who themselves experience the thicker sense of creative access to beauty. Radio has become the magic servant in this distribution of certain forms of beauty, the cinema of others, and television stands beckoning us on to the wonders of an age of science as it issues through martial victory into an epoch of peace. The cathartic quality of art, stressed long ago by Plato and then by Aristotle, the draining off of the malevolent emotions of men in ways mostly harmless and at times even beneficial, is available now for all men in ever-expanding volume. The problem novel and the crime story, popular forms of fiction in every age of high tension, is each a splendid example of this type of contribution of art to citizenship in general.

To sit, for example, under the reading lamp, in the quietness of one's home, and pursue the tangled web of human emotions in our hero for the evening, is to share with him our troubles and to gain from his predicament salve for many a wound. We get there the divorce to which our marital irritations prompt: we wash there our dirty linen in public; we deprive there our children of two parents and of intimate tranquility; we disturb there the texture of community peace with the raw materials for half-malevolent gossip; we enjoy there the new-found freedom of single blessedness again; and we marry there the next engaging object of our amorousness.

All this we do only to find in the closing pages, if the novel be true to man's tragic complexity, that the second—or is it the third or fourth?—venture into matrimony is no more doorway to idyllic felicity than the first. Finding through our hero that we ourselves are party to every domestic villainy, we subdue our waywardness at the door of action—and return to our commitments to realize that marital domesticity is not as bad as we had thought. Or do we? Such art makes such wisdom possible for modern men. This is one aspect of the catharsis of art. It is of the greatest significance to democratic citizenship, to have art that furnishes such easy catharsis to maladjustment.

Again: when the week has tightened our tensions to the breaking point, and the murder of somebody, if only of the System, alas, seems clearly indicated, we lie through the still hours of the night pursuing the impulse to murder through the pages of our favorite crime story. We do kill; we do get caught or spend weary years looking over our shoulders for the pursuers; and we do at last lay the book down with the murder purged from our hearts. Or do we? At least that is a function which such art performs for many and may perform for most. Thus to drain off major aggressions is a magnificent contribution to the peace of the community and to the calm of individual life. These are negative preparations for insight at last into the final form that beauty takes, a form as constructive as these forms are neutral.

For there is yet another way in which the benefits of beauty are spread wide in democratic citizenship. There is such a thing as institutional beauty, a form which heretofore we have ignored. Let us now see how our master, Plato, puts the matter, and then illustrate this benefit of beauty.

"He who would proceed aright in this matter," says Plato in the *Symposium*, "should begin in youth to visit beautiful forms; and first . . . to love one such form only—out of which he should create fair thoughts; and soon he will of himself perceive that the beauty of one form is akin to the beauty of another. . . . In the next stage he will consider that the beauty of the mind is more honorable than the beauty of the outward form . . . until he is compelled to contemplate and see the beauty of institutions and laws . . . and at last the vision is revealed to him of a single science, which is the science of beauty everywhere."

In this magnificent passage is opened up a preview significant in the extreme for democratic citizenship. Not until the institutions under which citizens live have taken on aesthetic meaning does citizenship come into its cultural own. The way in which the separate and even discordant impulses of men come to terms with one another, weaving a co-operative enterprise of egoistic impulses and endeavors, is also a process of art. Those who serve its progress are themselves makers of men and nations. Patriotism is itself a product not more of what nations are than of what citizens think and feel their nation to be. If all private visions of one's country get enmeshed into a seamless texture of imagination, citizenship has become a thing intensely spiritual and of dependable quality for the wear of peace as for the tear of war.

To this institutional aspect of the ideal, intangible but highly significant, we shall return in discussing politics as the discipline of goodness.

Let me, meantime, write this matter smaller than the nation by commenting first upon the aesthetic aspect of business and then by giving, in three scenes, types of reaction to the city as aesthetic material.

How could anyone look at a modern streamlined car, remembering how cars looked even a decade ago, without suspecting that American business is in no small part inspired by beauty? This might mean only that mercenary men see a mercenary value in catering to the aesthetics of a population. But it is hazardous to make it mean less than that business as an organization, if not most businessmen as individuals, serves in part the ideal of beauty. There is a pride possessed by businessmen, pride in the creative, that frequently overshadows the equally present and driving pride in "profits." Let me illustrate this at a lowly level by my story of the "Snake King of New Mexico."

During the Administration of President Calvin Coolidge —so the story was told me—the Tariff Commission was asked to institute a study of the differential cost of producing quails in Old and New Mexico, and to lower the tariff on imported quails if the difference of production cost justified such action. The sportsmen or consumers who had inspired the move evidently failed to show up at the hearing; for the Commission was reduced at last to questioning a man who had gone to New Mexico illiterate but was now somewhat improved, as the story indicates. He had discovered a commercial value in snakes, especially in rattlesnakes, and had grown opulent, in his own eyes, in the snake business. He had become in fact, Snake King of New Mexico. Finding that he knew little or nothing of quails, he was questioned friendlily as to his snake business. He let fall in the course of the questioning that he had lately forfeited a bonus of $500.00 on a consignment of snakes.

"What?" said the questioner in surprise. "Have you grown so rich raising snakes that you can sneeze at $500.00?"

"No," said the King, "it is not exactly that. I'll tell you how it happened. It was like this. When I received the order carrying the bonus, it stipulated that the consignment must be delivered that month, which was the month of February. When I started to send a telegram accepting the order, I did not know how to spell February."

"Surely," said the questioner, "you could have asked the telegraph girl how to spell it."

"What," rejoined our hero of business, "me, Snake King of New Mexico, ask a clerk how to spell a word? Why, I'd rather lose $500.00 any day. So I telegraphed that they'd be there in March."

This pride in the business community more often runs to pulchritude than to snakes, and it is a potent influence in recommending through diverse products the significance of beauty in human life, commercially and culturally. It could hardly be otherwise when one considers the aesthetic pattern adumbrated by a business community itself. Professor Alfred North Whitehead has put this matter in proper perspective in this discerning passage taken from *Science and the Modern World*:

"A factory with its machinery, its community of operatives, its social service to the general population, its dependence upon organizing and designing genius, its potentialities as a source of wealth to the holders of its stocks, is an organism exhibiting a variety of vivid values. What we want to train is the habit of apprehending such an organism in its completeness."

The aesthetics of business is, however, a long subject, and one to which we cannot undertake to do justice in this place. Let us turn, partly by way of introducing our subsequent discussion of goodness and politics, to a second illustration of the aesthetics of institutionalism. It concerns the city as a social unit. Let us note the progressive enriching of material and the progressive deepening of response as we pursue the theme through the three levels of our illustration, the poetic, the scientific, and the moral. To be concrete, we may suppose that my own city of Chicago—there are those who love her also—is the object of each of the cases, as she obviously is of the first.

I take a local poet's estimate—Horace Fiske—in order not to eclipse by the form of expression the latter two illustrations by the first.

> Born with the century's birthtime,
> Sheltered within a fort,
> Stripped of its roof by savages,
> At the river's lonely port;
> Driven by demons of whirlwind,
> And a million rushing flames,

> Smitten by anarchy's reddened hands,
> And a thousand deadly shames;—
> Still upward and onward, she marches
> With victory on her lips,
> With a dauntless eye,
> And a strenuous cry—
> To the world that she outstrips.

There the temporal pattern of the city, pegged down by a few dramatic events from her first hundred years of history, is spread before the mind. So to see Chicago is certainly more significant than to see it as merely the place where one lives and the place where one works plus the transportation between these two places. But it is not to see it as significantly as more detailed knowledge and deeper understanding would reveal it.

The same man or another man fresh from years of detailed study of the city, and yet with his vision still intact, recovers the city in imagination. Let the years have developed in him through unbiased devotion a noneconomic interest in economic processes, a noncompetitive interest in competition, a deep appreciation of the city for its own sake, as a variegated and absorbing pattern of multiform forces. Let such a man, I say, sit down in a calm moment and out of the colors at command paint in imagination the diverse elements that go to make a city: the physical habitat, the housing, means of transportation, the back country, different interests that form themselves into groups—social, economic, religious, political, educational—motifs all woven into the picture. Then let him animate this passive canvas with the pains and fatigues, the throbbing passions, the pulsing ambitions, the concealed inferiorities, the vaunted superiorities, the acclamations, and the resentments, that ever vivify the group life of man. Touch the picture to pathos with children playing in crowded streets.

Such a man will feel in greatly expanded form the fascination that captivates the simpler onlooker at a horse race, or a partisan at a football game, as the senses feast upon the colors and scents and expectancies fused into a complex whole. If he then endow this picture with a local habitation and a name—as I have—with memories, and a challenge to willing sacrifice, he will have illustrated my theme, the institutionalization of aesthetics. One who gets such a vision of institutional beauty for the first time will have found a day up to which will slope in significance most other days of his life and down from which, if he cannot maintain it, will slope many subsequent days. May we not, in fact, define the social scientist as one who has achieved and can maintain with consistency the aesthetic interest in some actual community?

Now let us take, finally and anticipatory of our subsequent discussion of the discipline of politics, our same man, or another with enlarged understanding of the city, and confront him with the demand that he stand for her mayoralty. Let us, you and I, constitute ourselves as the committee of his fellow-citizens to wait upon him, as is the wont in politics. Let us remind him that for such a city as that described in the preceding paragraph, the city of his home and of his heart, men have been glad to die in times of need, and let us lay upon him the higher honor, the deeper duty, of living for her in times uneventful. He knows that riches gained at her expense become ashes in retrospection; we do not need to tell him that her success through him would expand his own personality and fill full his cup of pride. It is not difficult for this committee—composed, as it is, of such competents as you and me—to sensitize him at once to the honor and the duty involved. Let us, with that clairvoyance you and I so easily grant ourselves, watch what happens inside him as he decides what he ought to do.

He—remembering our previous description of him—is probably not a professional politician who will with the greatest sacrifice easily lay himself upon the altar of his city and upon her contracts! Not being a professional politician, he will have a private job, business or position, for which he has been trained, in which he has succeeded, around which his friendships cluster, to which he also owes obligations. Without describing it, I wish here to ask you to elaborate in your own mind another pattern of these previous commitments as kinaesthetically rich, as personally appealing, and as morally exacting as the pattern of the city I have drawn to put inside his mind. Thrust your own pattern also inside his mind.

The man is now confronted by destiny, his own destiny; he is modest in the presence of fate. He must not only balance the goods, he must weigh against each pattern the evils of the other, which also are as rich aesthetic materials as the goods upon which we have concentrated attention. Both pictures are heightened by the call to action that involves renunciation of one alternative, surrender to the other. As these heightened patterns cross and conflict, merge or superimpose as he projects them alternately and then jointly into his future, rising now, it may be, with one to fame, sinking now, perhaps, through the other to oblivion—this man's mind as it moves to decision is the unbelievably complex and indescribably rich reflection of the institutional beauty which I present to you as the climax of citizenship. Informed with at least two configurations, either of which alone, the medium allowing, would become great art, marked by a struggle between them such as to involve not merely the patterns but the sealing of his own fate; intensified thus by the poignancy of having to sentence to death one honorable self and, without respite to mourn the dead, having to invest with the robes of action the new self brought to birth through irrevocable choice—such a mind, in such institutional setting, equals in immensity as it surpasses in grandeur the starry heavens of Kant's immortal epigram. It reflects the aesthetic essence of institutional clairvoyance, the very quintessence of the ideal of beauty for the art of citizenship.

Equally important with these business and urban illustrations, and more indigenous to America, is the way in which country life is shot through and through with beauty. Heir of what God has made as well as architect of what he himself may add, the farmer who takes his business as a way of life is indulger in, participant in, and beneficiary of a beauty immeasurable. Let us do our deference to the aesthetics of rural citizenship before turning to politics as means to goodness.

Those of us who have mixed the very soil with our fibres, how deeply in our bones we know that farming is an art and how it lifts life a notch or two if pursued as a way of life sensitive to beauty. Our farmer is but a man like other men, who breathes and eats and sleeps, with the normal mixture of grudges and more than the normal stock of good humor and homely cheer. But the farmer awakened is an artist at home in his world. It is from a farmer, a farmer in the Texas of my rural youth, that there ever echoes through my own farm-formed soul this smiling maxim for any day of troubles: "Anybody who'd complain at such and such," said he, "would kick at dying." Here is the beauty of piety so natural as to be cosmic in texture.

Who would complain at the weather, for instance, save a fool? At this goodly earth, save a grouch? At this old and lasting freedom of our American way, save a weakling and a cheat? The farmer complains but little at what he has found must be endured. He has long been disciplined at the fountain of necessity to drink whatever water nature yields. He has learned that it is not the lot of mortal man to live at ease. He, of all men, knows what is within human powers and what is not. It must be left, therefore, to men of lesser symmetry of character and piety of thought than the farmer to kick at dying or to fail to attune his course to that of the Cosmos. "Who best bear their mild yoke, they serve Him best." When we meet the farmer himself in person it is easy to sing in quiet key the homely sweets of his fruitfulness. Men of the city may be indifferent to his freedoms, but none can be for long indifferent to the fruits of his endeavors; for all must wear what the farmer grows, all must eat what he produces, all do share with him fidelity to our native land and joyous contemplation of our American skies of liberty. We yield to him and to his way of life the simple testament of beauty as part of our thanks for his age-old service to the nation.

The larger truth is that the earth was already old and mellow when early man planted savage foot upon the soil.

The first human act was, perforce, to make partnership with nature, pledging mutual troth under open skies. Fruitful was this early covenant between man and mother nature. The testament of its fertility is to this day corn and cotton, is pear and apple, forgetting not the luscious peach nor yet the royal watermelon red within as wine and many times more simply sweet. From this partnership with nature comes marrow for our bones and all sweet sustenance for our sinews. And from it, too, comes at its best a large and roomy sanity to clothe man's soul in peace.

It is a wise person who knows what must be borne and bears in quietness the genuinely inevitable. That is the farmer, nature's first and oldest child. It is a wiser person who sees of all our ancient woes what science can improve and so takes upon himself to remedy burdens men have carried long but need no longer bear. That is the progressive farmer, nature's last and strongest child. The farmer has the first and last of wisdom—resignation for the inevitable, remedy for the reparable.

Little wonder, then, that the old folly of romantic hope called Communism finds so little root on American soil. With all their hardships, our farmers have not lost their senses. The American farmer knows too well that wishing is not willing, that complaining is not remedying, that hope is extravagant folly when its roots are upside down. Trusting the turn of fate, as the Communist does, to usher in some classless society, he leaves our farmer cold. Every son of the soil sees for himself that horses vary in strength and excellence, that cows yield different qualities of milk, that hogs run from useless razorbacks to prosperous thoroughbreds. He knows too that men differ in willingness to work, in capacity to think, and most of all in practical ability to turn the bad into the better through quiet sagacity and lasting patience. Our farmer will not accept the run-around of romance founded on mere loose talk. Revolution is not a word of any magic down on the farm. No intoning of the phrase "dialectical materialism" solves a single problem, or adds an iota of contentment to the life of man. Propaganda does not make two blades of grass grow, but none at all, where one grew before.

Son of earthly sanity, the American farmer is too wise to be a radical. He knows deep down the painful price in patience which lasting progress takes. He knows the quick limit to self-indulgent hope, he who has wrestled with stock and stone and tussled with all forms of weather. Yet he knows too that the bad can at times be made into the better if men but pull together up the slow path of knowledge and down the hard, rough way of work. His sanity helps keep this nation sane against the pathetic illusions of foreign fanaticisms.

His sanity is indeed antidote to all the "isms" that beckon us from abroad. The braggadocio of Fascism leaves the farmer unaided for all its paraded pomp. The cruelties of Naziism but add man's inhumanities to the ancient burdens laid upon man by the maxim that he who will not work shall not eat. What will it boot the farmer, he asks, to generate hate among men from race or creed? Is life not hard enough without going out of our way to make it harder? What good does conquest do, asks the farmer, when it only adds empty pomp to problems already hard enough to solve or bear?

No; our farmer has little fancy for foreign fads. He

exemplifies an integrity so leveled down to the very ground that he is hardly touched by the churning of the fanciest ideologies, and never helped by the shortcuts of those hungry for power or fanatical of creed. It is not the least of debts this nation owes the farmer, thanks that his sanity serves as ballast to keep rigged and running our ship of state.

It is, however, no dead level of national life which the farmer illustrates and promotes. He is in this nation a factor dynamic as well as an influence conservative. He stands at once for both change and stability because he has found a way of life that in itself is good, and capable yet of betterment. From his backlog of dependable value he can reach for the better yet to be without letting go of the good that is. Each stage of his living and striving has meaning in itself, and yet each is a step to some importance coming on. He never has all that he needs, but he never has to risk all that he has. Thus it is that the farmer combines, as perhaps does no other worker, the staid and the progressive aspects of human existence. Under him he feels the stable earth, above him sees the steadfast stars. And all about he beholds in teeming multitude both animals and plants, alive with growth. He becomes participant organic in the ordered change of old earth's eternal seasons.

When, therefore, winter settles upon his fields, however heavy its hand, the farmer rests in confidence that spring will follow in its course. In cosmic trust, he readies himself for a new lease on effort and soon goes forth with his own energy replenished to meet the rising sap of weed and woodland and to harness for fruitful ends the animal friskiness of lot and barn. As spring slips into summer,

ART: THE DISCIPLINE OF BEAUTY

the farmer may lean back for a moment of respite to survey what he and nature together have made or marred. As summer passes into autumn, he matures into bounteous lord of the harvest or, as fate decrees, deepens his piety to accept once again the discipline of hope deferred. As the gods of the outer order call the turns of the zodiac, our lord of the land stands at each turn to do his part. To match thus with mood appropriate to each the succession of the seasons is to have became wise like the gods, knowing good and evil without surrendering to the pride of the one or to the blight of the other.

I dared forth one day to spy upon the census taker as he assessed the lot of one such son of toil. I would see for myself, I thought, whether with all its questioning, science can turn into figures cold the unassessable wealth and wonder of the open way. I had heard and more than half believed what the city saviors of the farmer were saying—that the farmer is ill-housed, ill-fed, ill-clothed; that he languishes for parity of purchasing power; that he must have hospitals, schools, roads. I had heard, too, what other city saviors of the farmer were saying, saviors intent upon saving the farmer from the first set of city saviors. They were saying that the farmer needs only to be let alone; that he is being regimented; that even the census taker himself invades the farmer's privacy and drives an opening wedge for later destruction of all our ancient liberties. I spied upon the census taker, I confess, to find what his job was like and to see for myself what government conceives to be the weal of the farmer's ancient commonwealth.

The farmer answered the prescribed questions as best he might. His children played upon the floor while they were turned by question and answer into ciphers. The blue-eyed baby, whose rollicking laugh from clean mouth made my old bones feel young once more, went in as a figure indistinguishable from other babies of dirty mouth and crying mood. Through it all I saw no rebellion on the farmer's part, only cautious reluctance as old and fine as character produced from daily contact with the soil. The questioner did not prod, and the answerer did not kick; nor did I find the two together conspiring to subvert our older way of liberty. All was done with decency and order, as knowledge grows from more to more.

But the philosopher in me reflected sadly that the ciphers would not be different from one another when statistical machines made the national pile complete. The poet in me made mental note, too, that no ciphers at all went in to mark the shy smile that passed between the farmer and his still pretty wife when her age was asked. The blue sky above did not get into the figures, nor the wholesome breezes from the meadowland across the way. And even the majestic oak in the front yard was ignored, though its leafy branches had no doubt transformed many a heated day into shaded delight; though its bark bore testimony to the childish joy of climbing; and though from its largest limb was suspended a swing that made my own heart palpitate to the long memory of "up in the air we go flying again, up in the air and down."

When science had finished with its questions, the census taker went on his way to swell these figures with other figures in our national assessment of material well-being. The politician waited at the other end to find from the figures what required immediate remedy, what might simmer for another decade untouched by oratory. By invitation I went with the friendly farmer as he rounded out his evening chores.

One of the cows that had just gone into a nation's assets was named Winnie, and as the farmer in passing called her by her given name, she stretched her neck to lick his hand for its pleasant salt. Yet the Government knows Winnie not. She might as well be "Moochie" for all the figures show. A young mule kicked at me when I got too near, but neither his mulishness nor my old Texas grudge against this beast got recorded in that book down the road under the enumerator's arm. Old Nellie whinnied as the farmer rubbed her underthroat; and he called her name twice over with the same-fibered affection, I thought, that had graced the fugitive smile to his wife when she hesitated to tell her age. No such affections, nor any shadowy recollections stirred in me by them, were enumerated as assets on this farm. Neither the runt pig which the farmer picked up tenderly nor the boar which he had to kick out of his way was marked down in the books of a nation as significantly different. They both went in as hogs. I noted, at the end, a pneumatic cushion on the tractor seat and in front of it an upright antenna through which flowed the news of the world as dusty acres were turned beneath the plow.

The farmer stopped a moment as we left the farm lot for the house, stopped and stood to mark, in silence, the afterglow of sunset. I had for all my city years forgotten the glory that gloaming can be in the country. I wonder, indeed, if I had ever in my whole life seen the sky so richly ruddy. The smoke in which we city dwellers live and move and have our being was altogether missing. Even the East had stolen the glories of its opposite, and yet left the West full-breasted in its pride and beauty. The farmer peered down the road at the now almost vanished census taker, looked again at the flaming sky, and turned to meet my contemplative gaze with what was hardly more than the sideswipe of a smile.

> We scarce had need of words at all,
>   As died that blessed day;
> The smile that lighted in his eyes
>   Said what there was to say.

4

Politics: The Discipline of Goodness

Politics ... is made up of unique situations in which a man suddenly finds himself submerged whether he will or no. Hence it is a test which allows us better to distinguish who are the clear heads and who are the routineers.—José Ortega y Gasset, "Revolt of the Masses."

WE COME NOW to the third and final value which justifies our liberty-way, given the appropriate discipline to beget goodness and to keep it dynamic. To be good and to do good, these are desires that rank with those motivating men toward truth and beauty. In a sense these may be said to lie deeper in our nature than those, but not so deep that we can trust the natural instincts of men to lead us to goodness any more than to truth and to beauty. Would that it were so, as it is so widely thought to be! Natural benevolence keeps us no nearer the fount of goodness than the hunger for knowledge, undisciplined, gives us truth, or the lure of art, undisciplined, gives us beauty. Goodness also is deeply a matter of discipline, a different discipline, to be sure, from either of the others but not less difficult and not less imperative.

GOODNESS ALSO HAS ITS DISCIPLINE

It was this imperative which Socrates had in mind in teaching that virtue is knowledge, vice, ignorance. He was led by his own observation, as each of us must be tutored by personal experience, to know that the noblest virtue may in the hands of the untutored yield the very vice it is set to oppose. For instance, take courage, said Socrates: in the hands of the overdisciplined it becomes cowardice and in the hands of the underdisciplined it becomes rashness. The ignorant mutilate virtue because they are not trained, as he put it, to discern "the grounds of hope and fear." Whatever the precise nature of the discipline required—and that we are presently to indicate—we may here affirm with the noble Greek that goodness does not descend upon men effortlessly like the dew from heaven. "All things excellent," to quote Spinoza (a third time), "are as difficult as they are rare." Goodness is indeed of so rare a vintage of excellence that it is worthy of all the pains which we shall now unfold as the condition of its life and growth.

In proposing politics as the name and nature of this discipline of goodness—just as science has been shown to be the discipline of truth, and art of beauty—I have enforced upon me by long experience the sense of proposing a paradox, if not, indeed, of perpetrating a shock. Politics, many, many good citizens conceive as a low enterprise never rising higher than moral mediocrity and not infrequently sinking as low as plain perversity. Surely, think they, men do not have systematically to suffer such an evil as politics that goodness may live and grow. Do I not now, indeed, overhear a multitude of our best citizens thinking a thought about their politicians as roguish as these lines by W. W. Montague are rollicksome?:

I'd decided to vote against Bilkins, though I couldn't exactly tell why;
I just didn't enthuse when he stated his views, and he had a mean look in his eye.
The speeches I heard him deliver seemed vapid and wobbly and weak.

"I'm off him!" I said with a shake of my head; and then I
heard Murkinson speak.
I said to myself as I strolled from the hall: "Bilkins might
not be so bad after all!"

Next morning I read in the papers a statement that Bilkins
had made,
Concerning finance and the possible chance of a speedy
revival of trade.
I read through a couple of columns of how he'd clean up
Wall Street,
And the way he'd proceed in this hour of need to set the
world back on its feet;
And I said to myself, as I sat there, said I: "Well, Murkinson can't be as bad as that guy!"

Next morning came Murkinson's statement of the ways and
means he had planned
To set us all back on prosperity's track, if ever he got a
free hand.
He said in a year at the farthest, and he thought it would
not be so long,
He'd have us all back on a smooth easy track and life
would be one grand sweet song.
And I said to myself, with a catch in my throat: "I'll ballot
for Bilkins—that is, if I vote!"

Experience counsels us all to treat with deference some such prejudice against politics as all but universal among moral-minded men. As the price of winning credence for my thesis, therefore, let me now do my deference to this disparagement of the art of politics. I shall begin with an example that will expose to its very roots the curious plant of politics.

Consider a present drive, coming to recurrent heads in Congress, the drive against our national wage-and-hour law.

This is a drive which is mercenary on the surface, but only on the surface. The shortness of the work-week seems to reduce output below the level of safe profit. When efforts are made to retrieve this loss and to increase production by overtime, the wages provision of the law doubles the profit hazard: time-and-a-half for overtime with wages doubled for Sunday and holidays. Mercenary on the surface, the drive is deeply moral at heart.

Yes, in the light of all the factors involved, it is disingenious to doubt the sincerity and sustained honesty of manufacturers and businessmen and of their elected voices in Congress. This honesty is complicated though not compromised in the South, whence its loudest voices arise, by a sincere agrarianism and a deeply honest resistance to the collectivization of labor which industry somehow brings in its train. And in both South and North the drive is further complicated if not purified by the sentiment of patriotism. How can labor loaf along, the patriots insist, on forty hours a week when their as well as our sons are at the command of death twenty-four hours a day seven days a week on the sea, on the land, in the air? And how in heaven's name, they persist, can labor haggle over time-and-a-half and double pay for holidays when our boys, deprived of arms thereby, thus have their dangers doubled—and that at what would be a peace-time pittance. A profit motif is here before our very eyes transformed into a moral cause pregnant with patriotic fervor.

This is a transformation, however, which—alas, alack!—is no respecter of persons. Look you now at the other side of the conflict.

The drive which passed this law and now seeks to sustain it is also mercenary on the surface, but only on the surface. The unequal access to leisure in a civilization dedicated to equality of opportunity has long been a crying shame. The shame was deepened by what appeared the collective impossibility to remedy the sister shame, the grossly unequal purchasing power in a civilization with an ever-rising standard of life. Why should not the men who do the body of the world's work reap their share of what they create and, failing that, why in heaven's name should they not be compensated by a larger leisure in a world where more and more is created by less and less? Clearly labor was out to get, and clearly is now out to keep, its largess in our ever-expanding prosperity. Mercenary on the surface, this drive too is deeply moral at heart.

For why not, why not labor with its wages swollen to absorb the ground swell of our national prosperity, or, that failing, with its leisure enlarged to pass the work around and to share the major psychic income from toil? Why not indeed? Is democracy a moral enterprise dedicated to equality of access, or an immoral one dedicated to monopoly of enjoyment? And as for patriotism, who in the last war was it that identified patriotism with profiteering? Is this "gang" now to be allowed to make patriotism the second refuge of economic scoundrelism? Thus the hidden thoughts of laboring men and the strident plea of their audible voices in Congress. And as for forty hours a week, let management, let bureaucracy show that they are producing more. Let the efficiency experts testify at what maximum of hours the maximum output begins to decline. Call the statisticians to testify whether there is a shortage of labor, save at the level of such high skill as will not be helped by increased hours or lessened pay. And, last of all, look at the marvelous morale reflected in labor's voluntary renunciation of the strike for the duration and at the remarkable speed with which we have bettered even the German record at converting a nation to full-bodied war.

It would surely be disingenious to doubt the sincerity and sustained honesty of laboring men and of those who defend the convictions of labor in the Congress of the United States. This honesty, like that of the other side, is complicated though not impugned by many, many factors. But it is confirmed by one everlasting fact, the fact that democracy is a moral impetus ever making for equality among men: first, for political voice, but at last for economic access to all the unearned increment of an age of science. War for democratic ends is a sounding brass or a tinkling cymbal unless it is furthered by men sharing in its prosperity as well as in its hazards. This is, after all, what the shooting is all about, or ought to be about—a *materializing* of the ethics of equal access all along the line.

These two sides, with swords clashing but with arguments never quite meeting, confront each other in Congress in every recurrence of the agitation over hours and wages. Each side has a material stake, but one which has been heavily moralized; and each cause alike is now drenched in patriotism. Equally honest men, with causes equally sincere, meet in such manner that neither side can permit the other to have its way without both loss of face and impairment of self-respect. That's politics.

And the first result of such meeting is that you, if you are relatively disinterested and want to know which is right or more nearly right, cannot believe implicitly what either side says. You certainly cannot believe what it says about the other side, and you cannot fully believe what it says about itself. Each side, out of a deep, even a desperate, sincerity, will fudge a little—like "Mr. Sludge," Browning's all-too-human Medium, who could not but do a little evil that great good might surely come:

> Why, here's the Golden Age, old Paradise
> Or new Utopia! Here's true life indeed,
> And the world well won now, mine for the first time!
> And all this might be, may be, and with good help
> Of a little lying shall be: so, Sludge lies!

And how easy, through the logical slipperiness of art, borrowed now illicitly from the field of beauty, to justify a benevolent Jesuitism—just like "Mr. Sludge, the Medium":

> Why he's at worst your poet who sings how Greeks
> That never were, in Troy which never was,
> Did this or the other impossible great thing!
> He's Lowell—it's a world (you smile applause),
> Of his own invention—wondrous Longfellow,
> Surprising Hawthorne! Sludge does more than they,
> And acts the books they write: the more his praise!

This is not really cheating—so our Sludge is arguing. It's "rationalizing," which at times to the best of men appears morality's reasonable service in a world too complicated for simple norms. In such a jumbled situation science cannot furnish us truth, though we sadly need it as touching the facts, for there is no way as yet of begetting agreement between groups in honest conflict. Each will call its own experts; and communication often becomes an exchange of blows. It takes no poet to make the procedure as plausible as daily practice—as it appeared to "Mr. Sludge, the Medium":

> Take plain prose—
> Dealers in common sense, set these at work,
> What can they do without their helpful lies?
> Each states the laws and fact and face o' the thing
> Just as he'd have them, finds what he thinks fit,
> Is blind to what missuits him, records just
> What makes his case out, quite ignores the rest.

That's politics.

Politics, then, is what you do creatively when goodness itself, or if you now better please, justice, is being undermined by the conflicting claims of equally honest men. Here arises the imperative of saving goodness from its claimants, lest with its demise both truth and beauty be turned into their opposites through the prostitution of science to propaganda, art to fiat. Agreement upon facts lacking, and lacking also all means of begetting agreement upon principles, politics becomes the procedure through which, and through which alone, a new formulation of goodness arises to save something claimed by both sides from the otherwise certain wreckage of each other's honest counterclaims.

With this contemporary example before us, and a poet's clairvoyance to render it plausibly moral, let us now begin at something like the beginning, to establish credence in our claim that politics is the rightful discipline of goodness and through goodness the patron of all other ideals. But this means to begin, as it were, where the moral life of man commences. We need to see what this conscience of man is like which spreads its tendrils over every claim and complicates conflicts by transforming every case of collective contention into a cause for which somebody or other will dare to die.

CONSCIENCE AS A DISGUISED BID FOR POWER

We each achieve near the beginning of life promptings, pro and con but mostly con, which come to be called by a single name, the honored name of *conscience*. We wish to be good, after the order of what we think that to require; and, becoming good, we wish to do good, after that personal pattern projected into social life. (Sometimes, of course, failing to become good, we "take it out" on others, overdoing with fanaticism on them what we have underdone with weakness upon ourselves.) We shall not carp at this moral impetus in collective life, since it is the way of things human. It is indeed well as long as it is the entire story. But the plot thickens—most rapidly.

For, look you how we do associate with us others who are as like-minded as possible, and especially so on moral matters. Each confirms the other in his promptings. We jointly agree upon conversion of other men, recalcitrant but available for conversion: available with tolerance if afar, for castigation if too near. That conscience is in part a power-drive is all but certain; I have argued in an earlier book, *Beyond Conscience*, that it is a power-drive altogether. But all or most a power-drive, conscience is conscience, present in the best of families and persecutory in far from the worst. To be moral means to be more or less intent upon making other people at least a little better than we are.

While we are engaged upon this mission, however, to the other-minded, the other-minded (who are like-minded enough to themselves) are doing it to us (who are the other-minded to them). Sooner or later such groups meet (for this includes all groups intent upon making the world different and better). Before they meet, they have all consolidated their forces, clarified their ideas, perhaps hired executive secretaries, certainly, at least, have sharpened their demands. Demands for what? you say. Don't I, for a fact, hear you asking me: "Are you implying that every moral man has an axe to grind, and that the demands of conscience are the recurring grinding of that axe in public?" "Yes," I reply, "that is what I am implying. But my tone of voice is not quite the same as yours—mine is more wistful, even more sad—made so by perhaps more political experience than you, with the moral-minded."

Let me explain how I mean it. Two (or more) groups meet at last. They are sincere. They are decided as to what justice, or honor, or plain decency requires. Each is decided, I mean—each decided somewhat differently! No one intends anything mean, but just the right thing, the *decent* thing, you know, under the circumstances; but each has a different notion both of "the circumstances" and of the "decent" thing. Either would yield on mere monetary differences (I am speaking of civilized men, remember). That is, they would yield upon such matters within reason (a different reason!); and neither would stand unalterably on pride, personal or professional (with a different notion of "pride"!). It's nothing merely personal or mercenary; it's "the principle of the thing." Yes, it's always the *principle* of the thing; that's all that finally counts between equally honest men.

It would take a poet, clairvoyant of the innermost recesses of the human heart, to tell this story with adequacy. But I must tell it with such clarity as I can. In the plainest prose, men wrap their consciences around their concerns, until whatever the contents of the claim may be, the form of the claim is moral. From the other's side it may look selfish; it may appear purely mercenary; it may, if persisted in, look like "pure cussedness." From the inside, however, its just demands are clarified by conscience and reinforced by association of the like-minded (on the matter at hand, at least). True, one may have to "cut the corners" here and there to make his own case appear impeccable, but never like the opposition, of course—whose conduct is admittedly (by one himself) outrageous. The final fact is that there is no important case of conflict over capital which is not also a conflict of consciences.

From this final fact, the moral is twofold. The first moral is that conflict is inevitable, and the more moral the contestants, the harder the conflict. Conscience consecrates the conflict into a cause, indeed into two causes! To get clear to the very bottom, this inexorability of conflict serves as preparation for the second moral, which is that mediation is required for a peaceful adjustment of these inexorable conflicts. Mediation is required because the amount of accommodation is more than moral-minded men can yield without a paralyzing sense of guilt. Some guilt is inevitable in an evil world, but there is a sense of guilt which impairs the self-respect upon which alone good citizenship can be founded. It is this degree of guilt which would attend necessary adjustments if men with the stoutest convictions had to meet each other and to unbend, without any saving of face at all.

POLITICS IS THE DISCIPLINE OF GOODNESS

Mediation, however, implies mediators; and to act as moral middlemen is a delicate matter. It requires some prevision, more circumspection, and not a little of institutional clairvoyance. It demands, for instance, a kind of conscience which can itself remain relatively clear while making its main business the muddying or at least the maddening of the consciences of men who admit they are much better than the mediators. This conscience must bear, like the scapegoat of old, the guilt of others—and do it without being oppressed by any guilty feeling. Mediation, that is, demands what we call "politicians," men who can compromise issues, even the most moral issues, without themselves being compromised thereby. This gets so complicated, however, that perhaps I'd better return once more toward the beginning and unfold this point systematically. Since, however, I have treated the matter elsewhere in detail—*The Promise of American Politics, The Legislative Way of Life,* and (with Leonard White) *Politics and Public Service*—I content myself here with a summary statement of the principle of politics, with emphasis upon the way politics serves as means to the high end of goodness.

Politics can be seen, in the context just sketched, to be the art, or science if you will, of settling disputes. If men do not want intermeddling with their business, then they have only to avoid serious disputes with one another. But this we have seen, and this we well know, to be impossible. Human variety itself begets different points of view; these give different views; different views develop through sincerity into contests, and contests deepen into conflicts. Politics arises as undisputed king of all that's in serious dispute. Men accept this accommodation, to begin with, in order to avoid accepting something worse to end with. Domination is, in the large, the only alternative to politics, when equally honest men are in deep difference as to what is good. Either one side gets its complete way, the other knuckling under—which is what we mean by dictatorship—or a new way is devised, which is the way of neither, in which each gets enough of what it wants to observe a truce in the spirit of sportsmanship—which is what we mean by democracy.

Politics, created as it is by dispute, is spread in influence by every growth in discrepancy and deepened by every confirmation conscience gives to capital. Where there are deep discrepancies between the claims of those equally honest, efforts to eliminate politics succeed only in supplanting politics in the good sense by politics in the worst possible sense. Indiscriminate disparagement of politicians as a type tends to supplant responsible politicians with politicians irresponsible. The radical efforts of our time to rid society of politicians altogether, as in Communism with its merely administrative state and as in Naziism with its *Führerprinzip*, succeed in supplanting replaceable and improvable politicians by politicians so absolute that they will not be improved and cannot be displaced short of suicide or assassination.

At worst, then, the democratic system (which, at its plainest, *is* just government by elected politicians) is superior to totalitarian systems in this regard at least, that we democrats can turn suspected rascals out while they must keep indisputable rascals in. All this mess arises at bottom, we shall not too often repeat, from honest claims by one group to what another group honestly disputes. In the wry reflection of Justice Holmes, all legislation is an effort to shift unwanted burdens from tired backs to unwilling shoulders. This scene-shifting of reluctance, which is natural and indeed inevitable, is social fate if accepted by citizens slavishly; but it is democratic opportunity if accepted by them creatively. Mutually counteracting claims can be treated creatively, however, only through some such moral mediation as that provided to conscience by the institution of democratic compromise.

Before emphasizing finally the discipline thus constituted by politics, we must see more clearly what is involved in each alternative: negatively, then positively. On the negative side, we must see that not to accept a compromise solution of honest conflict is to undermine the entire edifice of ancient justice. That means for the whole temple of achieved goodness to come tumbling down around our ears. Property rights pass; and *property* rights, it must be remembered, are *human* rights—in property. If out of natural social tensions a Hitler comes to power, any unliked class is dispossessed of its property: first, perhaps, the Jews; then, maybe, the Catholics; then, for all you know, the Protestants; at last, whether you like it or not, anybody and everybody whom the dictator despises, or the climate of opinion leaves out in the cold. The "intuition of the Volk," *as interpreted by the chief intuiter*, this vague thing substitutes for all that the ages have reared to render men secure from surprise and trespass in relation to things, to things upon which life itself at last depends. So it is in Germany, and so with this or that modification could it be, would it be, under any thoroughgoing dictatorship. This is the alternative in regard to property. It is all the negativity that democrats have ever known, further negated.

But property rights, I repeat, are human rights—in property. When these human rights are rendered insecure, other more intimate human rights are open to attack from the rear, from the flanks, and, in the event, brazenly in front. The privacy of homes is invaded, perhaps to search for *verboten* property, or to seek out the persons of those who, dispossessed of property, are by that fact deprived also of all personal security. Then freedom of speech is denied in the name of common safety. Disavowal of sanctity of person follows hard upon, for men who are not allowed to speak freely can be arrested on the charge of freely thinking what they are forbidden to say.

In the rapid revolution of arbitrariness, *habeas corpus* goes under. The right to bail upon arrest follows. The right to trial before peers passes into the wrong of being convicted by the simple device of being accused by a party member. All these rights being fled, anybody can presently be sent to a concentration camp whenever somebody pleases, and once within the hell hole, all the indecencies of a sadism worse than savagery can be perpetrated upon anybody by somebody. First property goes, then privacy, then all liberty, and at last what is hardly worth while without these, life itself, which is forfeited as though it were a worthless thing. Arbitrariness *may* stop short of any one of these stages of degradation, but it need not stop short of all of them. What need not be, seldom is, to the undisciplined. Discipline lifted, license alone is law. That is the alternative to the politics of compromise: the negatives of civilized men further negated into barbarism.

Let no one escape the full force of this alternative as touching the means to the ideal of goodness. Goodness vanishes when justice passes through caprice into cruelty.

Goodness in all its forms is the precipitate of a long-maturing discipline; and if that discipline is done to the death, not only does the career of goodness stop, but the fruits of its previous growth wither upon the tree blighted by arbitrary power. Every impulse to give refuge, every gesture of even simple neighborliness, even the friendliness of a passing greeting upon the street—everything which the notion of goodness socially connotes is forbidden the Germans in dealing with, say, the Jew. Such reversion to utter undiscipline can never be made to stop with one group, nor can it be arrested at the boundary of even the social. Just as it spreads from one group to another, so it spreads from without to within, from external command to internal corruption, leaving at last a heart careless of tender feelings and an imagination cauterized against all mercy. Thus comes the nihilism of goodness when conflicts are treated uncreatively.

In conflicts creatively compromised, however, goodness grows from more to more, while in us dwells more of reverence for all the fruits of justice already dropped from the ancient tree of goodness. As with truth, so with goodness; as with beauty, so with goodness—the safety of its old forms depends upon their being leavened constantly into life by the creation of new forms of justice.

This brings us sharply to, but does not yet fully confirm, our claim that politics is veritably the discipline through which new forms of goodness arise among men. Nor can we confirm a claim merely by attaching to it the question-begging epithet of "creative." Let us settle, therefore, now, to the positive task of showing how democratic compromise actually does furnish growth to goodness and keeps alive the goodness already precipitated as justice in our culture.

A SHINING EXAMPLE OF POLITICAL COMPROMISE AT WORK

Let us take as illustration a case old enough to emancipate us from the prejudices that still animate us all when wages and hours, for example, are mentioned. It is a case touching two heroic American figures, opposite in temperament and enemies in principle. It is a case which involved a moral conflict between them at a time when each was backed by a faction so strong that neither had the freedom of action which belongs to private individuals. It is a case, you will see, grown into a cause; a case of conflict at something like its worst, a case which could easily have given rise to dictatorship in America, as its similitude has repeatedly given rise to this elsewhere. It is a case, nevertheless, which was so settled as to illustrate fully both the fact and the fruits of what I have been calling a creative resolution of conflict. It was a resolution through the art of political compromise, with all the dubious trimmings of a "trade" between politicians.

I refer to the early conflict over what was called Assumption. It involved Alexander Hamilton and Thomas Jefferson as principals. It concerned the question as to whether the new, then very new, national government in North America should assume responsibility for the debts incurred in the Revolutionary War, and it spread to include the debts created by the several colony-states. It had long ceased to be a mere monetary matter, as all such questions cease to be. It had become a matter of first moment in terms of political principle and of national policy.

Moreover, it developed, as always appears, into a matter which implicated private consciences and complicated public business with individual senses of conflicting duty. We take it, too, at a period when it raised the question of the very safety of the Republic and at a juncture in that period where the parties were deadlocked in Congress, where deliberation had broken down to yield place to the voices of passion and the forces of disunion. There America had its first great, if not its very worst rendezvous with destiny. Jefferson himself tells the story (in "The Anas," *Works*, IX, 92-95), tells it so unsparingly of himself that one is disposed (apart from the obvious epithets at the end) to count the telling fair to the other side also:

Independently of the debts of Congress, the States had during the war contracted separate and heavy debts; and Massachusetts particularly, in an absurd attempt, absurdly conducted, on the British post of Penobscott; and the more debt Hamilton could rake up, the more plunder for his mercenaries. This money, whether wisely or foolishly spent, was pretended to have been spent for general purposes and ought, therefore, to be paid from the general purse. But it was objected, that nobody knew what these debts were, what their amount, or what their proofs. No matter; we will guess them to be twenty millions. But of these twenty millions, we do not know how much should be reimbursed to one State, or how much to another. No matter; we will guess. And so another scramble was set on foot among the several States, and some got much, some little, some nothing. But the main object was obtained, the phalanx of the Treasury was reinforced by additional recruits. This measure produced the most bitter and angry contest ever known in Congress, before or since the Union of the States. I arrived in the midst of it. But a stranger to the ground, a stranger to the actors on it, so long absent as to have lost all familiarity with the subject, and as yet unaware of its object, I took no concern in it. The great and trying question, however, was lost in the House of Representatives. So high were the feuds excited by this subject, that on its rejection business was suspended. Congress met and adjourned from day to day without doing anything, the parties being too much out of temper to do business together. The eastern members particularly, who, with Smith of South Carolina, were the principal gamblers in these securities, threatened a secession and dissolution. Hamilton was in despair. As I was going to the President's one day, I met him in the street. He walked me backwards and forwards before the President's door for half an hour. He painted pathetically the temper into which the legislature had been wrought; the disgust of those who were called the creditor States; the danger of the *secession* of their members, and the separation of the States. He observed that the members of the administration ought to act in concert; that though this question was not of my department, yet a common duty should make it a common concern; that the President was the center on which all administrative questions ultimately rested, and that all of us should rally around him, and support, with joint efforts, measures approved by him; and that the question having been lost by a small majority only, it was probable that an appeal from me to the judgment and discretion of some of my friends, might effect a change in the vote, and the machine of government, now suspended, might be again set into motion. I told him that I was really a stranger to the whole subject; that not having yet informed myself of the system of finances adopted, I knew not how far this was a necessary sequence; that undoubtedly, if its rejection endangered a dissolution of our Union at this incipient stage, I should deem that the most unfortunate of all consequences, to avert which all partial and temporary evils should be yielded. I proposed to him, however, to dine with me the next day, and I would invite another friend or two, bring them into conference together, and I thought it impossible that reasonable men, consulting together coolly, could fail, by some mutual sacrifices of opinion, to form a compromise which was to save the Union. The discussion took place. I could take no part in it but an exhortatory one, because I was a stranger to the circumstances which should govern it. But it was finally agreed, that whatever the importance had been attached to the rejection of this proposition, the preservation of the Union and of concord among the States was more important, and therefore it would be better that the vote of rejection should be rescinded, to effect which, some members should change their votes. But it was observed that the pill would be peculiarly bitter to the southern States, and that some concomitant measure should be adopted, to sweeten it a little to them. There had before been propositions to fix the seat of government either at Philadelphia, or at Georgetown on the Potomac; and it was thought that by giving it to Philadelphia for ten years, and to Georgetown permanently afterwards, this might, as an anodyne, calm in some degree the ferment which might be excited by the other measure alone. So two of the Potomac members (White and Lee, but White with a revulsion of the stomach almost convulsive,) agreed to change their votes, and Hamilton undertook to carry the other point. In doing this, the influence he had established over the eastern members, with the agency of Robert Morris with those of the middle States, effected his side of the engagement; and so the Assumption was passed, and twenty millions of stock divided among favored States, and thrown in as a pabulum to the stock-jobbing herd. This added to the number of votaries to the Treasury, and made its chief the master of every vote in the legislature, which might give to the government the direction suited to his political views. . . . When this sop played its influence out, another engine of dominance must be contrived. . . . This engine was the Bank of the

United States. All that history is known, so I shall say nothing of it.

Let no omission or commission of emphasis obscure from us what Jefferson did. His action represents fairly the price somebody must always be paying for democracy. It holds the secret of how democracy, established in idealistic revolution, can save itself only through realistic evolution. Without dishonoring what democratic revolution demands, it honors what democratic evolution requires. It explains both the downright honor and the reputational dishonor of the politician in democratic societies. Note what Jefferson admits that he did: he not only arranged a compromise which his friend White could accept only with "a revulsion of stomach almost convulsive" but he knowingly put into the hands of Hamilton the whole future fiscal policy of government, by making the treasury of the United States the patronage trough, as Jefferson regarded it, whereby Hamilton could and would become "the master of every vote in the legislature." One of the progeny of his compromise became the parent, as Jefferson saw, of that iniquitous child against which Jackson struggled, the Bank of the United States, and of that equally iniquitous grandchild against which Woodrow Wilson struggled, the monopolistic system arising from tariffs and other one-sided governmental favors. All this issues from Jefferson's own mouth to damn him and his breed forever as "low compromising fellows." Could honest John Cotton have made such a choice? Not likely. Could the highest minded of our day or of any day do it? Hardly.

Why, then, did Jefferson do it? How, then, *could* Jefferson have done it? How can the Jeffersons of our day, or any day, do it? Without being wise enough to say for certain whether Jefferson's estimate of the facts is accurate (the fact that Hamilton agreed with him as to the facts at hand is something in Jefferson's favor), we can discern what led him to the compromise and in some measure what have been its creative consequences. Jefferson was led to the compromise by fear otherwise of the dissolution of the Union itself. There are perhaps no first things—things, I mean, wholly beyond dispute—to which appeal can be made to *demonstrate* either that the Union was worth the price or that its preservation required such a price. But as beneficiaries of that Union we are not in a position to argue its worth. What have been the consequences of the compromise is clearer.

In the large, the Union was meant to be and has proved to be a system of two incommensurable but not incompatible principles: (1) the principle of compromise for the settlement of all weighty disputes, (2) the principle of no-compromise for the protection of all private principles compatible with public order. The preservation of the Union yielded the perpetuation of these two methods. The continuity of the sphere of privacy has yielded millions of us Americans down to this good day of immense population the priceless privileges of utterly free conscience, almost completely free speech, and a maximum security of body and property with a roomy field for psychic prowess. It has yielded this large return because it has perpetuated the compromise method of settling all serious matters publicly in dispute between men. The overt fruits of this preservation is that the method has given the Jeffersonians a chance in every generation to recoup peaceably the losses incurred by Jefferson to Hamilton at the prime.

If this compromise system had skidded upon the rocks of the first stern precipice, Jackson could not have struggled against the national bank—and yet there would have been a Biddle or his monopolistic double. If the system had failed, Woodrow Wilson could not have struggled against the same system of monopoly and privilege then dissipated widely rather than concentrated in a single bank. If the system had failed, there could have been no New Deal under Franklin Roosevelt to bring to equality in the competition for privilege the farmers and industrial laboring men. If Jefferson judged rightly of the dissolution of the Republic without his compromise, he purchased through that day's discipline all the good that subsequent years have wrought—and, to boot, the capital for Virginia!

I am not myself prejudging the justice of either Jackson's onslaughts against Biddle, or the New Freedom of Wilson, or the New Deal of Roosevelt II. I am, rather, celebrating the glorious privilege of those who did prejudge their justice to struggle with them against those who had other prejudgments in the premises. It is the justice of peace which I am prejudging, and of its methods of progress as contrasted with the retrogression of war. It is the fertility of discussion which I prejudge superior to the sterility of domination as a social method. It is the democratic way of life which I am prejudging, prejudging as better than the totalitarian way of death. It is the blessing of these which Jefferson foresaw and for which he was willing to sacrifice his capital without limit in war, his conscience within limits in days of peace. The demands of peace, no less than the tasks of war, furnish times that try men's souls.

POLITICS IN FULL SERVICE OF CITIZENSHIP

Given these prejudgments—with the Jefferson-Hamilton episode to illustrate their outworking—I pass now to the discussion of the disciplinary prices which our citizens must continue to pay for these means of creating goodness and, through the creative attitude, for the keeping alive and active of the old forms of precious goodness. Involved is great discipline on the part of (1) those who indulge in politics, and (2) those who participate in the processes of citizenship; and involved also (3) are great benefits to all as beneficiaries of this peaceful alternative to totalitarian violence in the settlement of inevitable conflicts.

Those Who Indulge in Politics

As politics is itself the discipline of goodness, so it is an enterprise which requires much preparation for those who indulge in it. There is, first, the discipline required to take a constant stream of criticism from those who admit themselves the best, and to return something less than evil for evil from those who are reprobated for their mediatory role. The volume of bickering, complaining, and reprobation which comes to one who holds public office in a democracy is not even faintly suspected by those who have never indulged in the responsibility of representing others when their dearest interests are at stake. Businessmen, says Donald Nelson, have tried and failed to stand the gaff. It is easy for politicians to grow calloused to criticism and even easier to become cynical under it. To know that one can never do anything entirely satisfactory for anybody, and yet to keep up courage and to maintain creative morale, this requires stamina of a peculiar and rare sort.

Even more stamina is required to deal with the thousand and one problems nearly every one of which outruns one's best information. The former demand requires patience, this latter requires courage as well as patience. To be constantly choosing between evils, as the politician must, in the hope nevertheless of making the evil chosen more bearable through the manner of its choice, is a drain upon the sort of optimism which is also required to do the job. To vote "yes" or "no" upon a thousand issues whose comparative merits in the press of business the politician cannot fully estimate, this is an adventure of faith. A legislator in a certain state was in the habit of prefacing even his affirmative vote with this formula, "with regret, disdain, and dismay, I vote aye." This may well represent recklessness to cover ignorance and laziness; but it may as well represent, as I think it did in this case, courage to choose the lesser evil and then to see it through.

To take an unending stream of criticism and at the same time to wreak oneself upon the problems at hand, which in no ordinary sense are even soluble, has always been the lot of one who represents equally honest and equally able men with interests in conflict. Hard as that lot has been historically, it is even harder today. The reason is not far to seek. As long as parties to the inevitable conflicts of interest were individual persons, the political task was limited in scope and more tolerable of fulfilment. That government was best which governed least, and "the least" was very little. Every matter in dispute was flanked by great areas of the customary not in dispute, and the dominance of the accepted was assured by the weightiest force in the world, the force of what was taken for granted, or on the negative side, the force of what simply "is not done."

Such was an epoch in which men were still just men, and corporations were all but non-existent. But, alas for political ease, we have lived to see an America with more than half a million corporations existent, and to see states granting charters for more simply for the revenue which incorporation fees provide. In such a changed world, of course, the spirit of the worker has fortified itself to confront incorporated wealth with unionized skill; and, of course, the courts have upheld what alone public opinion of changed times could countenance, the reasonableness of collectivism both among laborers and, now, progressively, among farmers.

The politician has thereby become, willy-nilly, the voice of corporative or at least co-operative enterprises larger than individuals but smaller than the State, and agent of the battle that sometimes seems to involve the whole forces of society in a single confrontation. Insofar as this occurs, the resounding clash of interests involves organically the remotest organizations of cultural influence and by the same token deprives the politician of the once comforting support of a large segment disinterested because uninterested in a given conflict. The new situation intensifies pressure *for* solution, but also permits pressure *against* the solution constituted by majority will.

The business of the politician remains, as it has always been, to serve as the custodian of the disputed, to create therefrom by acceptable compromise conditions for the resumption of relations along lines approved by public opinion, eventually to be sanctioned by new customs and supporting new moral standards. But the task is much harder to consummate and much harder to implement. The politician himself gets swept into the vortexes of general animosity, and there remains little neutral opinion left to back up whatever disinterestedness he can command. The settlement of disputes by compromise implies some undisputed ground as standing place for the settlement until it can take root in the moral consciousness created by its enactment. I do not wish to overplay this new difficulty in a corporate age; but that the politician's mediatory work is rendered very much more difficult by a frontal conflict developing toward a bi-totalitarianism of opposed opinions, is certain. Leeway required at the front for the proper discharge of his pacific role is ruined or hurt by lessened leeway at the rear and on his flanks. Those who indulge in politics must be more and more disciplined to stand the gaff and to turn it toward the moral creativeness described as its goal. The discipline requires tough skins to receive criticism, informed minds to get the facts in a thousand conflicts, and the ingenuity of personal charm to beget agreement from those morally reluctant to subject their consciences to the mediocrity of compromise.

Citizens Who Participate in Politics

If modern corporative conditions make harder the discipline for those who indulge—the politicians—it also makes harder the discipline for those who merely participate as citizens in the electoral and representative processes. The politicians are after all fortified by the unquestioned tonicity that is bred of the battlefield. They have the martial support of their partisans and of one another's mutuality. The optimism and good cheer of the average politician, even in defeat, attest to the high morale of those who indulge. One hardly finds a handful of the disgruntled among ex-congressmen or among the exes of that high turn-over of seven-thousand-five-hundred state legislators, most of whom are biennially elected or defeated. Those who are returned to private life return as dependable missionaries of the political process of accommodation.

Citizens, however, are always more or less disgruntled in all democratic societies. Disaffection increases as the corporate aspect of life intrudes more and more upon the form and fact of individual freedom. Individual citizens must more and more put their eggs all in one basket; and when that basket is manhandled, the breakage is high and the frustration deep. It requires no little discipline for citizens to stomach their politicians in a corporative age. The operation of what we may call the "Gresham Law of Politics" discloses the high need but the great lack of citizenly discipline. That law we may formulate as follows: *Politicians prodigal of promises tend to drive out of office politicians scrupulous of promises.*

The chief stumbling block, indeed, to what citizens most clamor for—i.e., better politicians—is very often the citizens themselves. Or, more specifically, it is the romantic expectations of citizens as to what may be achieved collectively, i.e., through politics. If citizens expect more than the process can yield, and if they vindicate their inevitable disappointments by electing men who will disappoint them

POLITICS: THE DISCIPLINE OF GOODNESS

still more, then democracy is on a toboggan heading for increased disillusion. Citizens must match the discipline expected and required of politicians with a discipline of their own.

This discipline requires, on the negative side, disparagement in advance of hopes based on man's collective life. It implies, on the positive side, enhancement of expectations from self-help and from cultural compensations. Rolling the two together before separating them for discussion, we may say that the worst thing possible for democracy is a too romantic citizenry. Such a citizenry will, out of disillusion with the gradual but in illusion with the revolutionary, follow this charlatan to the Left, that schemer to the Right, in full expectation of what lies neither in the green-looking pastures to the Right nor in the greener-looking pastures to the Left, but lies, if anywhere, in the hinterland of private endeavor or in the voluntary efforts of groups nonpolitical. Changing the figure, we may resort to the homely maxim of common prudence: in collective life only those who sleep on the floor never fall out of bed. To accept the floor is the first guarantee of continually enjoying the bed.

Discipline in citizenship, we have said, requires disparagement of all high hopes from collective life. Why men allow their hopes to run away with their reason when they think in collective terms is an interesting speculation, but we must here content ourselves to state what seems to be a dependable fact. This fact is, that high hope based on collective endeavor cannot be fulfilled because high hope conflicts with high hope. The best men moralize their hopes, as we have seen, and so make it their duty to maintain them against other men energized by an equal sense of duty to their hopes. Not to see this bottom fact is to lack sales resistance to the Pied Pipers who profit from what we have just described as Gresham's Law in Politics. To see this is to begin to achieve the discipline required of those who participate responsibly in democratic citizenship. Without this clarification we have no way of getting men to accept the discipline of disparagement in order to escape the penalty of disillusion. Disillusion leads to disparagement of the deeds of those who indulge rather than to discipline of the hopes of those who participate. The best deeds possible cannot withstand that disparagement, whereas the best hopes can helpfully suffer that discipline. Proper disparagement of romantic hopes will prevent disillusion altogether.

Knowledge of the best that can be achieved in collective life is that which enables one to accept the highest common denominator of private consciences as his public duty, even though it prove from his private point of view the very lowest common denominator of ideality. It is to enable one realistically to accept the least of two evils with the same stamina that in better times would lead one to choose the best of all proffered goods. It is to discern the wisdom of Thomas Paine's advice: that the infidel of democratic times is not he who disbelieves but he who professes to believe what he does not really believe. Children may believe, but grown men must be disciplined to doubt Pied Pipers who pipe what common sense so sagely declares to be "too good to be true." Adult citizens only profess to believe them, only "will to believe" them. This they do in the half-hope that their faith will create facts of the dimly discerned fiction. Citizenship should be made of sterner stuff.

If participation in political life requires, then, on the negative side, this discipline of collective disparagement in order to prevent wholesale disillusion, it also prescribes, on the positive side, a discipline to live alone and like it. The highest ideals are uncorrupted only when not subjected to compromise. A man may worship the trinity of truth, beauty, and goodness, beholding them in all their uncompromised purity, as long as he does not ask or permit other men to tell him what they mean and so to water them down to what both can agree upon. Let a man, therefore, prize privacy if he would maintain the purity of his ideals. And yet the discipline is not quite as austere as that sounds. There are always the like-minded for confirmation and enjoyment. There is hardly a man who does not have at least one friend in whose complacent face the original form of absolute ideals are reflected back to him untarnished. It would be only the impossible idealist whose devotion to the ideal would shut him up to pure solipsism. From this single and solitary friend, the community of the like-minded grows, or may grow, without assignable limits, outwardly toward a universal community, or at least toward a "choir invisible" who in ideal immunity from corruption share our moral convictions.

This discipline of contemplation would come into full joy if men could only be weaned from the superstition of believing that the best test of the moral ideal is the logical universal. That superstition foregone, citizens would forego self-assurance through proselyting and would find self-assurance where alone it is: in the utterly individual. To extend the community of the ideal is always to dilute the purity of the ideal. To accept the snugness of the completely private is to find our truth true, our beauty beautiful, our goodness good. If one cannot content himself with solitude, then he forfeits absoluteness of the ideal and tries to substitute therefor absoluteness of power, so that he may compel other men to agree with him. This he seldom if ever achieves in fact. Absoluteness is what men start with; they end with it only when they end where they began. To demand that absoluteness be shared is to invite others to substitute their notion of it for your notion of it, or is to deplenish both in compromise. Democracy does not require, or permit, agreement on fundamentals.

The discipline of solitude, however, is so much harder than the discipline of sharing that we can hardly expect men to be willing to pay the price of utter privacy for absoluteness. This value is so precious, indeed, that a little of it goes a long way with all gregarious animals. The discipline of citizenship is, then, more realistically the price of accepting compromise as the best possible in politics, and the like-mindedness of voluntary groups as a modified form of the absolute. While to "internalize laissez faire" is the fullest way to preserve freedom, as the world goes collective, "to acculturalize laissez faire" is a fair way to preserve what freedom indeed requires, governmental inroads into what yesterday was private business. Though the private possession of external goods is lost, however, not all of freedom is by any means lost. So long as men own their own bodies, they control an empire of intimate worth. Even if this empire goes under, not all is gone under. So long as men can forefend cruelty from themselves and can command without shame the simple joys of the sensuous, so long can they share some ideals without utter loss. They do not have to share all of them with everybody, but only those involved in political compromise. More of their ideals they can share with lesser communities than the state, and in this sharing can actually achieve enhancement of their freedom. To share with like-minded men what is not lost but rather found more fully thereby is a noble substitute for what laissez faire once meant. This is what I mean by "acculturalizing laissez faire." And then to keep to oneself what is so sacred that it must remain absolute—this is what I mean by "internalizing laissez faire."

The necessity of making common the means of distribution and the growing necessity of making political the means of production, these valid demands of a crowded world render not less but more necessary a pride in cultural things and contentment with one's solitude. To turn over to politics and the principle of compromise all that which for one man to have more of means for another man to have less of is not insuperable loss of liberty. To find one's chief joy and pride in that domain where for one man to have more does not mean for other men to have less is to have found a substitute in personal freedom for the larger liberty of laissez faire. It is to find autonomy in whatever one prizes enough to want to keep to himself; it is to find fulfilment in whatever one can share with the like-minded; and it is to find economic sustenance for both in a communal management of what is a precondition of all life and all living. It is, moreover, to be on one's way to what is more than mere tolerance for variety; it is to be at last on the road to an enjoyment of variety as an end of life.

To have the freedom to make absolute what one's own integrity demands; to have the privilege to expand personality by sharing all that can be shared with the like-minded; and to have the grace to accept good-naturedly in the field of the necessarily shared the best that political compromise can effect: this is to have all the fruits of democratic citizenship. This is the lot of all the citizens in a citizenship that has become genuinely democratic. It is, however, a concentrated residuum of the heavy dose of discipline which we have been delineating. Having delineated the discipline, let us here at the end celebrate without restraint its luscious fruits.

All Citizens Enjoy More Fruits than They Create

The first fruit bequeathed to all citizens of a democracy is peace. By disciplining ourselves into the notion of compromise, we get a majority settlement of all issues that survive the cultural efforts to universalize like-mindedness. If the majority has to impose its rule, the society is still motivated by fear and will be frustrated in spots. Even so, it is better that the majority have its way than that a minority have its way. Still the imposition upon a minority of the will of the majority is good only because it is barely the best of two evils. Peace thus achieved is indeed better than constant war, but it is only an oasis of order in a desert of potential disorder.

A long step toward the full ideal of goodness is taken when the minority itself accepts the rule of the majority as its way for the time being. This gives a breathing spell in which, through magnanimity, majority rigor may be transmuted into leeway for all. If good humor accompany the exercise of majority strength, the opportunity is afforded the minority itself to become a majority and thus to work its own good-humored will upon the dethroned majority. Whoever loses under this peace, loses in such manner as to retain the hope of winning again. From forbearance of such enemies as this rule assumes, arises appreciation of enemies as an added element in the spice of life. The processes of peace come to include whatever of war is necessary to social life: the very principle of revolution itself gets institutionalized; and peace consistent with progress has become a permanent possession of such human association.

This is the first great fruitage for all citizens of the multidisciplined way of life.

The second fruitage is like unto it.

From such peace arises freedom for all. This freedom is, as I have said, first the chance for minorities to become majorities. But this is the outer trapping of opportunity. I do not say this to depreciate order but to enhance inner contentment. For the final fruitage of peace is expansiveness of soul. Outer compulsion makes us brace ourselves against it until through dis-ease tensional tumors develop within us. The only way to maintain full inner health is to operate under conditions of outer harmony. A genuinely free individual can thrive only in a free society.

By the outer process of political compromise, therefore, and by it alone, is brought to birth an inner life free of compromise. By applying a second-best principle to second-best things, we find that the things of first moment can remain secure under the principle of perfection. Compromise for the compromisable—freedom for the indispensable. This is the final harmony between the political doctrine of accommodation and the moral doctrine of autonomous integrity. A man is not a good man who will compromise the core of himself, compromise, that is, the final principles by which he lives. But a man is not a good citizen in a democracy who does not meet other good citizens halfway. The good man and the good citizen meet and merge in a society so peaceful that freedom of conviction is habitually permitted but never perpetrated. This is the end-goal of the democratic way of life. A great philosopher, Immanuel Kant, has indeed described the final freedom and the last freedom of man as the self's legislating for itself—and for no one else.

By accepting compromise in things that count for least, we achieve autonomy in things that count for most. The dignity of man is thus safeguarded by a price which no dignified man need hesitate to pay. Our way of life requires exactly this wisdom to distinguish first things and then courage to keep first things first. The final preservation of the privacy of person and the right of conscience requires a mind very scrupulous in observing distinctions. If one claim as a right of conscience the power of suppressing other consciences, he not only loses the right of his conscience but compromises all his other rights with it. If one insist that right convictions about economics or about religion are matters for him to determine for others, then others when they grow strong enough will determine these for him. The only way to preserve any bill of rights is to be abstemious in presenting to the public the bill for what one calls his own rights.

Here, then, we find the first two indirect benefits of the discipline of politics—outer peace and inner freedom.

The third benefit arises from a combination of these two. It is to crown peace and freedom with institutional beauty. The thought of beauty that rises above the pulchritude of persons is neither radical nor new. We have already, in discussing beauty, quoted from Plato a marvelous passage on the beauty of laws and institutions. We may now develop that thought in a context appropriate to our finale, returning gradually to the obscuration of categories common to daily living.

The loveliness of laws is indeed a final form of beauty and a noble form of goodness. It tops the benefits of a political discipline; for it makes goodness self-regarding, something to be contemplated in its own right as well as something from which to expect continuous fruitage appropriate to cultivated men. It is parent of many a lesser form of worth, and godfather to other types of value beyond the strictly aesthetic. From it issues both goodness and utility, and athwart its course cuts now and again the career-line of truth. Where democratic laws prevail, their rigor being righted in the souls of men by good-natured acceptance, every virtue may thrive. Where there is not this prevailing majesty of the majority, no virtue can thrive save precariously. Truth gets Goebbelized and beauty Hitlerized.

Here in the discipline of politics is indeed somehow the final integration of the public and the private dimensions of life: the realm of political compromise weaving its garments of peace, and the realm of personal integrity working its way toward man's perfectibility. Inner ideals must work themselves out into public effectiveness, or all progress is blocked. Outer accommodation must work its way into the souls of men or else conscience becomes fanaticism and spreads its cursed blight over all the fair world of enhanced variety. Unless free course can be furnished the influence of each of these upon the other, each loses its significance and beauty. Where it can be furnished, we have free men operating in a fair society.

You will see how I am mixing my categories at the end, as I begged you not to do at the beginning. It is not inappropriate now for us to relax together toward common sense, where every form of value somehow involves every other form and so overlaps in discourse. Politics becomes, in this generous context, the gateway to every fair end. Where it does not flourish as compromise, truth goes under to propaganda, beauty is subject to the whimsical judgment of any one in authority, and the daily turn of kindness and neighborliness gives way to cruelty and then to a fearful savagery. The tolerance which a politics of compromise breeds is the *sine qua non* of the pluralistic values which democracy enshrines.

Let me cite therefore in conclusion the address of an American who, in singing his political swan song, rolls all values into a common eloquence. He illustrates the unity of virtue in a sportsmanship without which no virtue can live or any magnanimity develop.

Senator Henry F. Ashurst, after nearly a third of a century in the Senate of the United States, arose from his seat on September 11, 1940, and read into the *Congressional Record* this telegram which he had just sent to the aspirant who had unseated him in the primary election:

Heartiest congratulations upon your victory. You will make splendid Senator, and when Congress adjourns I shall come home to campaign joyously for you and the entire State ticket. I wish for you health, happiness, and political success.

And then Senator Ashurst spoke in brief part as follows:

Mr. President, I shall not waste any time on such miserable twaddle as to say that I ought to have been elected. A man only moderately versed in statesmanship, and with only a small degree of sportsmanship, is bound to admit that in a free republic, in a government such as ours, it is the undoubted right of the people to change their servants, and to remove one and displace him with another at any time they choose, for a good reason, for a bad reason, or for no reason at all. If we are to remain a free people, it is the duty of public servants not grumpily and sourly to accept the verdict of the majority, but joyously to accept that verdict; and I joyously accept the verdict of my party. . . . I should be lacking in frankness, I should be disingenuous if I failed to say that they probably had a fairly good reason for displacing me. . . .

A great many people unwisely imagine that the beauty and serenity of life inhere in office. No, Mr. President; royalty and honor do not necessarily inhere in cabinets, congresses, and courts; royalty and honor inhere in the citizen. Honor of itself does not reside in office; honor resides in the man. The great things of life are not signed and sealed before a notary public. . . .

When my present colleagues are here worrying about patronage, worrying about committee assignments, and about the scorching demands of constituents I shall possibly be enjoying the ecstasy of the starry stillness of an Arizona desert night, or viewing the scarlet glory of her blossoming cactus, and possibly I may be wandering through the petrified forest in Arizona, a forest which lived its green millenniums and put on immortality 7,000,000 years ago. Enjoyment and ecstasy arise in human life from the contemplation and appreciation of such things.

That spirit is the final fruit of the disciplines which make possible the liberties and the beauties of democratic citizenship.

Index

INDEX

Adolescence, 6-7, 61, 63, 126
Age of Reason, 35
Agreement, 24 ff
Anderson, Sherwood, quoted, 7, 53, 69, 71
Arbitrariness, 107
Aristotle, 73
Art, discipline of beauty, 51 ff, 68 ff
Ashurst, Henry F., quoted, 130-132

Bacon, Lord, quoted, 42
Beauty, 51 ff, 70 ff, 129 ff
Belief, 23
Berlin, vii, 10
Bonar, Horatius, quoted, 12
Browning, Robert, quoted, 99-100

Catharsis, 73-75
Chesterton, G. K., quoted, 24
Chicago, 78-82
Citizenship, science for, 41 ff; art for, 69 ff; politics for, 116 ff; romantic, 121
City, 76 ff
Civilization, 39
Clifford, W. K., quoted, 23, 27, 39
Collective action, 8, 123
Compromise at work, 109-116, 127-129
Conflict, 101 ff, 128 ff
Congress, 95 ff, 130-132

Conscience, 101 ff, 128 ff
Coolidge, Calvin, 76
Corporations, 118 ff
Credulity, 35
Czechoslovakia, 10

Darrow, Clarence, 36, 37
Darwin, Charles, 56-57
Dayton trial, 37
Debate with Nazi, 10
Democracy, discussed, 19, 20, 39, 41, 105 ff, 116
Des Moines *Tribune,* 29
Dickinson, Emily, quoted, 33, 51, 52, 59, 65-68
Diplomats, ix
Discipline, decadent, 3 ff; dynamic, 3, 12, 41; negatives of, 8 ff; of politics, 27, 80; of doubt, 34 ff; of art, 51 ff; of science, 54 ff
Dryden, John, quoted, 64

Educators, 45, 71
Eliot, George, quoted, 31
Emerson, Ralph Waldo, quoted, 58
Exhaust hypotheses, 26 ff

Farmers, and beauty, 82 ff
Federal Council of Churches, 25-26

INDEX

Fiction, 39, 73
First World War, vii
Fiske, Horace, quoted, 78-79
French Revolution, 35
Führerprinzip, 15, 105
Fundamentals, in democracy, 116

Galileo, 32
Gasset, Ortega y, quoted, 93
Goebbels, 16, 129
Goodness, 13, 93 ff, 103 ff, 108, 126
Gresham's Law of Politics, 120, 122

Hamilton, Alexander, 101 ff
Hartmann, Nicolai, 10
Henderson, Neville, 9
Hitler, 16, 104, 129
Holme, Jamie Sexton, quoted, 55, 70
Holmes, O. W., quoted, 32
Holmes, O. W., Jr., quoted, xiv, 33, 40, 42, 43, 47, 66
Housman, A. E., 61
Hutchins, Robert M., quoted, 6
Hypotheses, 54-55

Imagination, 4, 59, 69-70, 79-80
Infancy, 4
Infidelity, 36
Ingersoll, Robert G., 36

Jefferson, quoted, 109 ff

Keats, John, quoted, 12

Laissez faire, 124-125
Lamb, Charles, 63
Legislative investigations, 36 ff
Lowell, James Russell, quoted, 14, 67

Mediaevalism, 6
Meredith, Owen, quoted, 13-14

Montague, W. W., quoted, 94
Morehouse, D. W., 28-31
Morehouse comet, 29 ff
Mr. Sludge, the Medium, 99-100

Nazi "red cap," 35
Naziism, 10
Nazis, 15
Nelson, Donald, 116
Nietzsche, 42

O'Keefe, John, quoted, 13
Order, 11 ff

Padua professor, 38
Paine, Thomas, quoted, 36, 122
Pasteur, Louis, quoted, 27-28, 43; mentioned, 70
Peirce, Charles S., quoted, 38
Perfectibility of mankind, 18
Perfectionism, 6-8
Plato, 12, 72, 73, 75
Politicians, 105, 117-119
Politics, discussed, 26, 94, 100, 104, 118 ff; as discipline of goodness, 93 ff, 103 ff, 116 ff
Pollock, Sir Frederick, 7
Prague, 10
Property rights, 106 ff
Pumpkin pie, 61
Punch, 18

Religion, 24-26, 106
Roosevelt, Franklin D., 115
Roosevelt, Theodore R., 35

Santayana, George, quoted, 32, 39, 61-63
Science, discipline of truth, 23 ff; fruits of, 33 ff, 47-48; selection for, 34
Scientific caution, 26-30
Scientific saintliness, 34
Shakespeare, 13

Skepticism, 34, 38, 45
Smith, Russell Gordon, quoted, 3, 5
Snake King of New Mexico, 76-77
Socrates, 93
Solitude, 33, 123 ff
Specialization, 20, 40
Spinoza, quoted, 3, 53, 94
Sublimation, 72-75
Symposium, 75

Tennyson, Alfred, quoted, 36
Tough-mindedness, 44 ff
Truth, discussed, 12 ff; conditions of, 24 ff

Unamuno, 55
Unitarianism, 26
University of Chicago, 36
University of Texas, 36

Variety, 19 ff, 126

Wages and hours, legislation of, 95 ff
Wahlgreen investigation, of U. of Chicago, 36
White, Leonard D., 104
Whitehead, Alfred North, quoted, 78
Wolf, Robert, quoted, 48

Youth, x

www.ingramcontent.com/pod-product-compliance
Lightning Source LLC
Chambersburg PA
CBHW030115010526
44116CB00005B/254